Audio Access Included 🔊

HARMONICA
AEROBICS

BY DAVID HARP

Contents

To access audio visit:
www.halleonard.com/mylibrary
Enter Code
7751-8976-5200-2074

Cover Illustration by Birck Cox

ISBN 978-1-4803-4466-2

HAL•LEONARD®
7777 W. BLUEMOUND RD. P.O. BOX 13819 MILWAUKEE, WI 53213

T0057519

*This book is dedicated to my friend Paul Van Stavern,
who turned me on to blues and rock harmonica. Without his gift
of a J. Geils record – yes, it was that long ago – and a Sonny Boy
Williamson #1 record, I would still be playing "Taps" and a few
folk songs. Or, more likely, I would have given up the
harmonica before I knew what it was made for.*

*In addition, I would like to thank the Reverend Ardys Van Stavern
and the late Alice G. "Gene" Van Stavern of Wisconsin for so
generously providing me with one of my dearest friends.*

In Australia Contact:
Hal Leonard Australia Pty. Ltd.
4 Lentara Court
Cheltenham, Victoria, 3192 Australia
Email: ausadmin@halleonard.com.au

Visit Hal Leonard Online at
www.halleonard.com

INTRODUCTION

What Harmonica Should I Use?

This method has been created for use with two different standard ten-hole harmonicas. These are also known as "diatonic," "Richter-tuned," or "blues" harps and come in a wide range of models and prices. The two different harmonicas you'll need are a relatively low-tuned "key of A" harp and a mid-range "key of C" harmonica. Most of the earlier material in the book is for the key of C harmonica, since that's the key most players are likely to have already. Later material, featuring the technique known as "blow bending," will be demonstrated on the A harp.

How to Use This Book

Some of us like to get our information through reading, some from hearing, and some from a combination of the two. You know what works best for you, so you'll soon discover your own balance between listening to the exercises on the accompanying audio tracks and reading about them (including the notation) in the book. Your current level of playing, your ability to "bend" notes, and your ability to read standard music notation all play into this. However, once you have the hang of using *Harmonica Aerobics,* you can deploy it the way that feels right to you.

As soon as you begin using this method, listen to the solos section (Weeks 33–42). These examples are intended to demonstrate a variety of ways to approach a particular style of blues, rock, country, or jazz music. Hearing, for example, the 16-verse solo based on the funk/rock two-bar chord structure you'll learn to play in Week 1 will help you create solos of your own.

What follows here are some chunks of important information you may need, depending on what you already know. Read – or at least skim – the parts that apply to you.

If You Can't Read Standard Music Notation

Although you can learn the timing of the exercises from listening to the audio, taking a moment to understand the different note symbols used to indicate rhythmic values will speed your progress. (See page 89.) If you can't read music, no matter your level of harp expertise, start with the beginning exercises. The rhythms of these early etudes are simple (they use only single-beat notes called "quarter notes") and will make learning the notation easy.

Additionally, harmonica "tablature" – a simple arrow-and-number notation system showing which hole to breathe in or out on, and when and how much to bend notes – is written beneath each line of standard music

notation. It's described on page 94 of this book. It's okay to read only the harp tablature for each exercise while you listen to the audio demonstration, if that works better for you.

For Complete Beginners

Are you a complete beginner? If you don't know how to hold your harmonica and are not able to breathe in and out to play at least a few simple blues or rock "riffs" (combinations of notes you like and memorize), try my *3 Minutes to Blues, Rock & Folk Harmonica* book/audio (Hal Leonard, HL14036996) before reading further. An hour spent with that package will save you many hours – and you'd rather play blues and rock harp than play catchup. (Of course, if you've already bought this book and, especially if you are able to read standard musical notation and harmonica tablature, go ahead and give it a try.)

About Playing Single Notes and Chords

Some early exercises can be played using chords. A *chord* is a sound made by playing more than one note – usually two or three notes, on the harmonica – at the same time. It's easy to do on the harp just by keeping your mouth open wide while you play. What's harder, for beginners, is to get single notes. There are two main ways to do this:

With the *pucker method*, we make a small hole with our mouth, almost as though we were whistling. With the *tongue blocking method*, we cover four holes with our mouth and block the three higher holes with the front and side of our tongue. I believe that "puckerers" find it easier to bend and "tongue blockers" find it easier to use the advanced tone technique known as "octave blocking." Some players say tongue blocking produces better tone, but respiratory system control has more to do with tone than how one gets single notes.

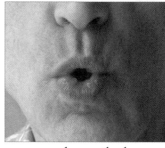 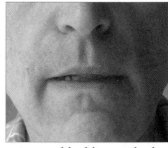

pucker method   tongue blocking method

Bending Notes

After learning to get single notes, *bending* is the most important (and difficult) harmonica technique. To bend a note, we create a specific tongue position while playing that note – usually on either the draw notes from holes number 1 through 6 or the blow notes from holes number 8, 9, and 10. The simplest bends will commence in Week 12. This means the earlier exercises won't sound as interesting or "bluesy" as the later ones – but those who can't bend yet will be able to use them. More advanced players who don't know much theory will also find important information in them (although presented in the form of exercises that are simple, technique-wise). To learn a little more about bending, visit BendingTheBlues.com or HarmonicaNoteBending.com.

MUSIC THEORY

A band often cringes when a harp player comes up to the stage and wants to "sit in," because harmonica folk are frequently stereotyped as not knowing music theory. Unfortunately, this is sometimes true, since many are self-taught. And it's not that hard to learn to play some blues and rock harp – especially when you are playing by yourself – without knowing any theory at all. So what? Well, jump up onstage and start playing your harp in the wrong key and you'll soon find out. If you're lucky, you'll be booed off the stage – booted off, if you're not! This is not a theory book, but you'll find a few helpful bits of theory instruction along with the exercises – as well as one crucial chart (see page 93) – that will keep you from ending up in the bad situation just described. If you'd like to be better versed in this subject, try my popular book *Music Theory Made Easy* (Hal Leonard, HL14022398). And knowing "just enough" theory will help you improvise – i.e., create your own original harp music – spontaneously.

Chord Progressions

Chord progressions are created by playing two or more chords, with each one played for a specific number of beats. We'll start out (page 8) with one of the simplest ones: a two-bar funk/rock chord progression. A "bar" or "measure" in most blues or rock music refers to a four-beat chunk of music. Each verse of a two-bar funk or rock chord structure is made up of two different chords, which are often written as Roman numerals: the I (one) chord and the IV (four) chord. The IV chord is sometimes played with an extra note, which turns it into a IV7 – i.e., a "seventh" chord.

A chord progression is like a skeleton on which a piece of music is built. At its simplest, each of the two chords (and remember, a chord is made of multiple notes sounding together) is played for four beats (or one bar). This is repeated until the end of the song. Beats of silence are sometimes used during each bar, as in Exercise #5 in Week 1. In a band, the chord progression is usually maintained by the bass player or the rhythm guitarist or both. But sometimes, when we play by ourselves, we have to keep the chord progression in our mind only, which is why I "harp" so heavily on memorizing the important ones.

Harmonica Theory ("Positions")

Over the past hundred years, we blues harp players have come up with our own version of music theory called "harmonica positions." Although this was developed by players who knew little or no standard music theory, the harmonica "position" refers to the particular "scale" you are using to play a piece of music. (We define scales on page 11.)

There are 12 possible positions, but seven are rarely used; you can learn them from my book *Blues & Rock Harmonica Made Easy* (Hal Leonard, HL14004667). Each uses a completely different set of holes and bends. However, many blues and rock harpists play mostly in "cross harp," more formally known as second position. All serious harpists should be able to play in first position and third position as well – and play at least a song or two in fourth and fifth positions (and a bit of sixth, for playing jazz). But for the first part of this method, we'll stick to a simplified version of the most common blues harp blues scale: the cross, or second position, blues scale.

For Experienced Players Who Can't Bend Notes

If you can play lots of melodies but can't do much with a blues or rock tune, you may not understand second position or "cross harp." Some of the exercises may seem overly simple, but it's still worth your while to work through the book from the beginning. At the same time, you'll need to start learning to bend; if you are good at playing single notes, this will be easier for you than for beginning harp players. For this, I recommend my book *Bending the Blues* (Hal Leonard, HL14003902).

For Experienced Players Who Can Bend Notes Pretty Well

If you already understand some music theory (such as scales and chord progressions) and harmonica theory (harmonica positions), you're in great shape to get the most out of this book. Skim through the earlier weeks and you'll soon reach material that will challenge you and add new riffs and positions to your playing. Many of the harder exercises use "partial bends," so if you can't already play three distinct bent notes from your harmonica's 3 hole, and two distinct bends from the 2 hole, keep working on your bending chops.

For More Advanced Players: Are These Exercises Too Easy for You?

Use a metronome. That's one way to hone your playing skills while practicing an exercise you might be tempted to dismiss as "way too easy." For example, the Simplified Second Position Blues Scale Exercise (page 11), or the Simplified Second Position 12-Bar Blues Solo #1 (page 12) might be boringly simple with the metronome at 90 beats per minute (bpm). But if you crank that metronome up much past 300 bpm, either becomes a good training exercise to keep your notes clear and crisp at high speed.

More advanced folk should skim through the earlier exercises and work only on those that seem useful. Want to play blues scales using high notes? Or use the 3 draw triple bend better? Want to improvise four-bar rock ballads? Just find those exercises. Eventually, you'll reach the hard stuff.

LIPS AND LUNGS, HANDS AND TONGUES

All the exercises will help you build muscle (and muscle memory) in one or more of these four main physical realms of the harp player.

Hands

Obviously, you have to hold your harp to play it (unless you're playing along with another instrument like guitar, bass, or keyboard, in which case you use a "harmonica rack"). However you hold your harp, and whichever hand you use, you need to create an enclosed space on the non-ten-hole side of your instrument by using the hand not holding the harp. And you need to open and close that space at will.

Generally, we call the sound made by doing this the "hand wah-wah." It's a wonderful tone technique.

My favorite basic hold – harp in left hand, with right used to open and close the open space – is pictured here.

Since everyone's hands are different sizes and shapes, experiment to find the most comfortable and effective way to get your hand wah-wah. Once you do, use it a lot. Even many experienced players use the hand wah-wah in a fast, fluttery way on notes held for a long time. But developing the ability to do one hand wah per beat – or two or three – will add excitement and emotion to your playing. Listen to songs from my old mentors Sonny Terry and Big Walter Horton, or check out Sonny Boy Williamson (#1 or #2) for examples of great hand wah-wah use.

Mouth Muscle

Whether you get your single notes by puckering or tongue blocking, you'll need to strengthen the muscles that encircle your lips: the obicularis oris. Play a lot; that's the best way to do this. Some of the articulation exercises, in which you'll be playing fast, clear, multiple notes per beat, will be especially good exercise for your lips. A student once referred to this type of exercise as "sending Morse code with your tongue." That's not a bad way to describe it.

Decide whether or not to let your cheeks puff out when you hit blow notes. If not, strengthen your buccinator muscles, which hold your cheeks in. How? By holding your cheeks in when you blow out, of course. This is only a matter of appearance, because letting the cheeks puff out doesn't affect tone or performance. It's your call on this.

Toughening the Tongue

Your tongue is an incredibly intricate organ made up of ten separate muscles. Four of these are extrinsic muscles; that is, they are attached to bony parts of your head. But six of them are intrinsic muscles, connected only to each other. In this way, your tongue bears some similarity to an elephant's trunk (though smaller and less complex). But it can move around, contract and expand, and hump and hollow in ways an arm or leg never can.

Learning to bend harmonica notes well is the best way to exercise the muscles of your tongue, as discussed at great length in my *Bending the Blues* book. Any of the exercises involving bending – and especially the more complex later ones – will increase the strength of your tongue and the degree of control you have over it. In most of the articulation exercises, the tongue is used to break the inhale or the exhale into short, crisp, individual notes. These will also exercise the distal (front-most) muscle portions of the tongue.

Your Respiratory System: Not Just the Lungs, but the Diaphragm, Too

Most people, when asked what the respiratory system consists of, would reply "the lungs." Yet our lungs themselves have no muscles. They are simply containers to hold and process air. The diaphragm muscle – that large, plate-shaped muscle that divides our body nearly in two – provides most of the power to inflate or deflate the lungs, aided by a few sets of chest muscles.

When playing, try to breathe "from the stomach" (more precisely, from the diaphragm). That is, as you inhale, allow your stomach/lower lung area (not your chest/upper lung area) to expand outward fully before you even begin to bring air up into your chest/upper lung area. When you exhale, do the opposite. Empty the air from your chest/upper lung area first, keeping your stomach/lower lung area filled until all the air is out of the chest/upper part of your lungs.

It may help to pretend your hands are glued to your stomach, middle fingers against your navel. Imagine your hands pulling your stomach out as you begin to inhale, keeping it puffed out until the very end of your exhale – then finally, when all the air has left your chest/upper lung area, pushing your stomach back in to empty your lower lung area. This, of course, will take practice – especially to do without thinking about it! But even trying to breathe from your stomach will improve your tone.

The Nasopharynx: Keeping Your Nose Closed

Another area most of us don't think much about is the connection between our nose and our mouth, known as the *nasopharynx*. Think about blowing out a group of candles on a birthday cake or sucking a thick shake through a straw. Neither is possible to do if you are allowing air to move in or out of your nose. Practice both if you're not sure whether or not your nose is closed. Remember to breathe from your diaphragm when you're practicing.

The Glottis: Machine Gun Sounds and Harmonica Tone

The glottis refers either to the folds that form our vocal cords or the space between them. To feel your glottis, say "Uh-oh!" loudly. Your glottis shuts and opens: shuts for the "uh" and opens for the "oh." This is called a *glottal stop*. Try saying a series of percussive "uhs" – "Uh! Uh! Uh! Uh!" It's like a kid making a machine gun noise: a series of fast, crisp glottal stops. We'll use this in our articulation and a fast series of glottal stops – sometimes on an inhaled note, sometimes on an exhaled note (both in and out from the diaphragm, of course) – providing the harmonica tone effect called "throat vibrato."

GOT RHYTHM?

Can you feel the basic "beat" of a song after listening to it for a few seconds? Do you think you have a good sense of rhythm? If so, no problem. If not, it's still no problem, as the earliest chord progression exercises should help develop your ability to hear the beat. The "skeletal structures" in Week 13 will also help, especially if you play them until you can hear them in your sleep. Learning to do the exercises that use parts of beats (like eighth notes, triplets, and 16th notes) will hone your rhythmic sense even further.

IMPROVISATION

Learning to *improvise* – to create decent (or great) sounding music spontaneously – comes to different players in different ways. Even though it's outside the scope of this book, it's an important topic to think about. (I go into the subject in *3 Minutes to Blues, Rock & Folk Harmonica* and *Instant Blues Harmonica*, HL14016094),

Some musical geniuses (Little Walter and Sonny Boy Williamson #2 are two good examples, among others) are able to improvise freely without knowing much music theory. They have tremendous control of their instruments and know what sounds good. They often play the same song in different ways. (For example, compare Little Walter's famous "Juke" with some of the "Juke" out-takes from the same session.) Other wonderful artists, such as Sonny Terry or Sonny Boy Williamson #1 tend to play rather similar riffs and solos over and over, but they may have so many variations you don't notice it until you've listened to dozens of their songs.

Unless you have tremendous innate musical talent, understanding scales and chord progressions – and being able to play them effortlessly, emotionally, and without thinking, in all different timings and note combinations – allows you to try out different things while playing, without going too far wrong. (If you don't make mistakes sometimes, perhaps your improvisations could be a little wilder!)

Whether or not you have great innate musicality, you'll still need to have good control over your instrument to express the musical ideas and feelings you have. The exercises in this book will give you that control, provide the structural and scale-related building blocks of improvisation, and allow you to better hear what the great players are doing. That last element is crucial: *Listen* to your favorite blues and rock harp players and learn from them.

–David Harp

About the Online Audio

On the title page of this book, you will find a code that allows you to access the online demo tracks. To hear a performance of a given example, refer to its exercise number. You can listen to the demo tracks online or download them to your computer and/or mobile device.

In Week 1, we'll learn some of the most important chord progressions. Since we'll play them using chords rather than single notes, this will give time to practice to those who can't yet play single notes well. As mentioned earlier, the rhythm will be simple, using only quarter notes (one note per beat). This will help those who aren't used to reading standard music notation, giving them a chance to get used to it. Again, we're starting off with a C harp, so use that instrument until otherwise noted. Remember to listen to the more advanced solos in Weeks 33-42 (Examples 205-214) while you work on the basic chord progressions that underlie those solos.

Exercise #1: Two-Bar Funk or Rock Chord Progression (Bends: None, Position: 2nd)

This simple but satisfying chord progression is used on lots of songs. Here, we play each chord for three separate beats, followed by one silent beat (or *rest*). We'll use 1-2-3 draw for the I chord, and 4-5-6 blow for the IV chord. When reading music, look for the Roman numeral chord symbols above each bar, even if you don't really know what they mean. These will help you identify common chord progressions. Make sure you can recognize the squiggle (𝄽; quarter rest) that represents the beat of silence. You'll see it, and its relatives, a lot. Once you can play this, try doing one single hand wah per beat (see "Hands" section on page 5). Note: The double bar lines with two dots at the end of this example are *repeat signs* (see page 95), which tell you to play the music twice.

TRACK 1

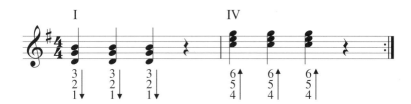

Exercise #2: Two-Bar, Three-Chord Rock Chord Progression (Bends: None, Position: 2nd)

This mellow chord structure adds a v chord (a lowercase Roman numeral indicates a *minor chord*, as opposed to the *major chords* we've heard so far) and plays each chord for only half a bar (two beats). In my *Harmonica-Based Mindfulness™* courses, I call this "The HarMantra™" since it is so useful in helping us focus on our breathing. It's used for many songs, including "Louie Louie" and "Wild Thing." Try to get your lungs relatively full on the draw chords and empty on the blow chord. Then play the chord progression at different speeds.

TRACK 2

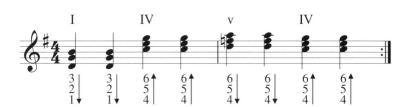

Exercise #3: The Eight-Bar Country Chord Progression (Bends: None, Position: 2nd)

Eight bars (32 beats) long, this one uses the same three chords (I, IV, and v) as Exercise #2 but in a different order. It's used by songs as different in style – if not chord progressions – as the country ballad "The Wreck of the Old 97" and the main parts of the Rolling Stones' "Honky Tonk Women." There are two new elements: the use of a two-note 4-5 draw chord in bar 4 and the second half of bar 7, and a two-beat note (half note) followed by a two-beat rest (half rest) in the last bar. A little later, we'll learn a scale that fits this chord progression like a glove.

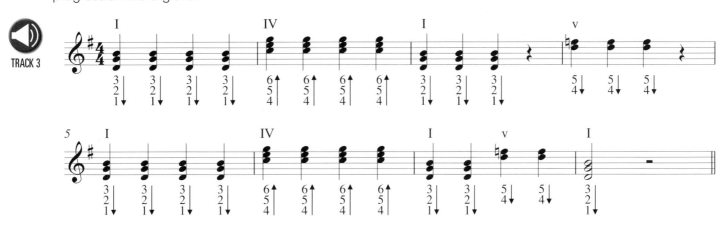

Exercise #4: The 12-Bar Blues Chord Progression (Bends: None, Position: 2nd)

This is the single-most important chord progression for blues harp players and, with slight variations, for rock 'n' roll harpists as well. The three chords – the I (one), the IV (four), and V (five) – are used in a specific order. The last bar of this exercise forms a turnaround. A *turnaround* reflects the fact that the last bar of this type of structure is usually a V chord. It's a slight change in the music (here in the form of a 1-2 blow chord and a single-note 1 draw) that helps announce that one verse is ending and another is about to begin. Not all blues solos have a turnaround, but many (if not most) do. It can last from two beats to two bars.

Note: In a normal blues, the V chord is major or dominant (like a major but with an extra note, the 7th, to produce more tension), but we can't produce this on our diatonic harp in 2nd position. The v chord we can play (and have been playing) is a minor chord. While this sounds good at times, it clashes at others. When in doubt, play a single-note 4 draw, which produces the "root" of the V chord only, which will work with any V chord (major, minor, dominant, etc.).

If you don't already know this chord structure, listen to it until you can hear it in your sleep. It's that important for blues and rock players. Memorizing the chords of this 2nd position structure will also help you "feel" when the chords change, so when you're playing alone, you can still maintain an accurate 12-bar structure.

Got Single Notes?

From this point on, many of the exercises use single notes. If you're a near-beginner, this doesn't mean you have to be able to hit any hole, at will, as a perfect single note. But you should be working hard on this if you can't do it, even while you continue through the next exercises.

Exercise #5: Single Notes Funk Rock Riff (Bends: None, Position: 2nd)

The following funk/rock four-bar exercise will help you work on "getting single," but it won't sound awful if you don't do a perfect job of it. It will also assist with the important 6 blow to 2 draw jump and serve in learning single-note versions (called *arpeggios*) of two important second position chords: the I (2-3-4 draw) and the IV (either 4-5-6 blow or 1-2-3 blow – these are the same notes, only they're in different *octaves*). See the Harmonica Notation Legend on page 94 if that's confusing. Until we can bend notes well, we won't be able to play the full IV7 chord, but a IV chord will work fine for now.

TRACK 5

More Complex Chord Structures

In later weeks, you'll learn chord progressions that are either more complicated (such as the 32-bar "AABA" jazz chord progression) or require single notes (like the four-bar rock ballad). For now, the 12-bar blues, a slight variation of which is also used in rock music, is the one to practice and memorize.

WEEK 2

In Week 2, we'll learn to play simplified versions of the most valuable scale a blues or rock harpist should know, as well as two less commonly used ones. Single noting will become more important, so if you have not mastered (or at least worked on) that, please do. After we've learned the "simplified blues scale," we'll finish the week with two easy and recognizable 12-bar blues solos.

What's a Scale?
A scale is like a musical alphabet. We use the letters of an alphabet give us the basic building blocks that we combine to form words and sentences and paragraphs. When we use the 26 letters of the English alphabet as our basic building blocks, we produce words and sentences and so on in English. If we use the 33 letters of the Russian alphabet, we produce words and sentences and long novels by Tolstoy. The musical alphabet, however, contains only seven different letters: A-B-C-D-E-F-G.

Exercise #6: The Easiest Major Scale (Bends: None, Position: 1st)

You're probably already familiar with the major scale, our childhood "do-re-mi." It tends to produce upbeat, happy sounding songs – from Beethoven's "Ode to Joy" (Symphony No. 9) to "Mary Had a Little Lamb." In its simplest form, it's not very useful to blues or rock players. But more advanced versions provide a great way to practice certain bends and make it easier to play advanced first position blues and rock harp. Also, since you've had it drummed into your head since childhood, it's an easy scale to start with if you can't already read standard notation. (If you can read standard notation already, skip it.)

C Major Scale

Exercise #7: The Easiest (Dorian) Minor Scale (Bends: None, Position: 3rd)

The minor scale produces music with a sadder, more plaintive sound. (There are two main variations most important to harpists: the Dorian and the Aeolian.) If a song has a melancholy sound, like "Greensleeves" or "Eleanor Rigby," it was most likely written using the notes of a minor scale. (It's less often used, however, than the second position blues scale in Exercise #8. Once we learn this Dorian scale, we'll be able to instantly morph it into a third position blues scale.)

Exercise #8: Simplified Second Position Blues Scale, Up and Down (Bends: None, Position: 2nd)

To create blues music, we use – you guessed it – the blues scale. But to play even the easiest real blues scale, we need to bend notes. In the following early exercises, we'll do simplified versions of the second position blues scale. To complicate things, there are three conventional ways to produce harmonica blues scales (and two less common ones).

You need to be able to play this from low note to high, and from high note to low – even though it won't sound bluesy until you can bend a little bit. This is a crucial skill for all beginning blues or rock players. If you can already bend, go straight to the "real" cross/second position blues scale on page 57. But don't forget to return to this page for lots of useful exercises.

Tip: Before you practice this simplified version, check out the real thing: Exercise 139 (page 57). Then return to this page, informed and ready to work toward the actual Blues Scale, once you know how this simpler one corresponds to the real thing. Intermediate players can practice this with the metronome at increasing speeds. Play it repeatedly. Practice this scale both by itself and along with the four-bar funk/rock backing.

Exercise #9: The Simplified Second Position 12-Bar Blues Solo #1
(Bends: None, Position: 2nd)

If you've practiced the previous exercise, you're ready to use it along with other musicians in the simplest possible way. In the following 12-bar blues solo, begin by playing the previous exercise twice. (This provides you with eight bars of the solo.) Then add a slightly revised version (also four bars long, with one different note at the end), below, so that the last bar acts as a turnaround. Voilà! You have a simple 12-bar solo that will sound okay as long as you are playing along with 12-bar backing.

Exercise #10: The Simplified Second Position 12-Bar Blues Solo #2
(Bends: None, Position: 2nd)

The previous solo doesn't make much musical sense when played without background musicians or recorded music, since it does not indicate when the chords of the progression change from one to the next (except for the turnaround bar). But if we use each bar of Exercise 9 separately, we can create a solo that works with or without backing music.

WEEK 3

Of course, we don't have to use all the notes (in pitch order) of the simplified blues scale in our solos and riffs – which, as you may recall, are combinations of notes we like and memorize. We can choose a few notes – not necessarily those next to each other, once we learn to jump accurately – add a bit of rhythm, and then memorize them for use in solos. *Jumping* is an important technique, but not all that exciting.

In the exercises that follow, the first note is a dotted-half note. In 4/4 time, a dotted-half note gets three beats. Tap your foot in time to help you keep a steady pulse. Practice these etudes for a little while and then move on, coming back if it seems useful.

Exercise #11: Easy Partial Blues Scale Riff without Single Notes
(Bends: None, Position: 2nd)

Near-beginners: Are your lips sore from trying to play single notes? Following are a few good-sounding riffs that use two-hole chords. You'll notice we use a 5 blow note; it's not a blues-scale note, but it works because most of the rest of the notes are. (I'll explain more about this later.) Do it twice in a row. Start empty!

TRACK 11

Exercise #12: Easy Partial Blues Scale Riff without Single Notes for IV Chord
(Bends: None, Position: 2nd)

This is the same rhythm, but reversed breathing – inhales become exhales. When you play a 12-bar chord structure, this will sound good during bars 5–6. You'll hear it, soon enough.

TRACK 12

Exercise #13: Easy Partial Blues Scale Riff without Single Notes for V and IV Chord
(Bends: None, Position: 2nd)

Again – same rhythm, different notes, but it will work fine when we play it in the right place.

TRACK 13

Exercise #14: Easy Partial Blues Scale Riff with Single Notes for Turnaround
(Bends: None, Position: 2nd)

Exercise #14 is the same as this week's riff, but in the last bar we jump from the 3-4 draw to the 1 draw, which helps the listener hear that the 12-bar form has come to an end. Yes, the 1 draw is a single note, but it's an easy one.

TRACK 14

13

Exercise #15: Easy Partial Blues Scale 12-Bar Solo (Bends: None, Position: 2nd)

Six riffs at two-bars per riff equals one simple but acceptable 12-bar solo. (Upon closer inspection, you'll see that there are only three riffs, because bars 1-2, 3-4, and 7-8 are the same.) Composers and improvisers often create "thematic solos" in which many of the riffs are repeated as variations of the main riff. (In this case, the main riff is stated in the first two bars.)

TRACK 15

Exercise #16: The 2 Draw to 4 Blow Jump (Bends: None, Position: 2nd)

Practice this slowly until you can do it accurately. You may want to do it with the metronome tracks, starting slowly and speeding up as your jump control improves. We'll use it in the following riff.

TRACK 16

Exercise #17: The 4 Draw/6 Blow/4 Draw Jump (Bends: None, Position: 2nd)

This is another important jump to know, but since it's the same distance on the harp as the 2 draw to 4 blow, it should be easy – as long as you start on the right note.

TRACK 17

WEEK 4

This week, we'll do two different types of exercises. We'll forget about chord structures and single notes for a bit and learn two of my favorite simple train songs. "Trains," especially if you're a near-beginner, are a fun and easy way to play something that sounds good and can be expanded into a great solo showpiece, as we'll do in later exercises. If you're an advanced player, trains are an excellent etude for breath and tongue control – if you do them along with the faster metronome tracks.

Soon we'll add the simplified blues scale to our trains; it's a great way to practice while walking down the road, with no need to worry about structure. We'll also begin to work on a specific form of the 12-bar blues, the boogie woogie.

Exercise #18: The Simplest Train with Trill (Shake) Whistle (Bends: None, Position: 2nd)

Notice the "play 4 times" indication, as well as the trill (or shake) symbol over the whistle part, which you'll play twice before repeating the entire piece as often as you like. Experiment with how often the whistle is used, as your train seems to need. Move smoothly from the 4 draw to the 5 draw and back. Do it as quickly as you can, while getting reasonably clean single notes. It may take some practice. Speed it up if you like, as in the recording.

Make sure you're ready for the jump from the "train wheels" (1-2-3 blow) to the "whistle" (4-5 draw). The jump back to the wheels is made easier by the quarter rest.

TRACK 18

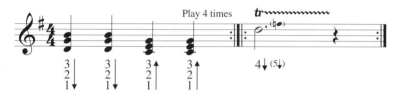

Hint: If you've worked on your trill, go back to Week 3 and add trills to the long chords (three beats each) in Exercise #15: Easy Partial Blues Scale 12-Bar Solo. Trills will work especially well on the draw chords.

Exercise #19: The Pre-Swinging Train (Bends: None, Position: 2nd)

This train is similar to the wonderful locomotive motif Charlie McCoy ("The Fastest Harp in the West") uses in his version of the classic country harp showpiece "Orange Blossom Special." It introduces the use of the single hole 1 draw note. Slant the high end of the harp away from your mouth if you're not yet a good single-noter. Again, speed it up if you like, as in the recording.

TRACK 19

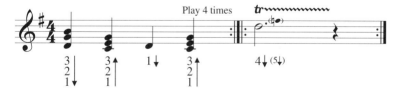

Exercise #20: Three-Chord Boogie Woogie Prep Work (Bends: None, Position: 2nd)

This simple four-bar chordal exercise will prepare you for a boogie woogie solo that soon follows. It also sounds good by itself, sort of like an expanded and slightly mournful version of the two-bar three-chord rock progression played as a solo. Boogie woogie is a style of 12-bar blues music that comes from a popular New Orleans piano-playing style of the early 20th century.

TRACK 20

15

Exercise 21: The Turnaround

In addition, practice this simple turnaround bar:

Exercise #22: Easy Chordal 12-Bar Blues Solo (Bends: None, Position: 2nd)

Creating an improvisation from the notes of chords is a perfectly acceptable way to create a 12-bar blues solo, but it will be much more exciting if you can use bends. Notice the turnaround: the last bar, ending on the 1 draw. This is good practice for near-beginner readers and will help prepare you for a boogie woogie 12-bar blues.

Exercise #23: The Boogie Woogie 12-Bar Blues (Bends: None, Position: 2nd)

This 12-bar blues adds a non-blues scale note (5 blow) to the previous exercise and begins our study of the important boogie woogie style. We'll use a turnaround – 6 blow, 5 draw, 4 draw – taken straight from the blues scale. Learn to play this well, and you can take the place of a rhythm guitar or bass player in a jam session – for a few songs at least – and let them do some soloing.

WEEK 5

This week, we'll add eighth note (half beat) rhythm and note variations to the simplified second position blues scales and use them in a 12-bar blues solo verse. If you can't already read standard music notation (or at least standard music notation rhythm), these exercises will help. By the way, creating "improvised" solos from memorized riffs may not be the deepest form of improvisation, but almost everyone does it sometimes – even the planet's best harp players. Listen carefully, for example, to Little Walter's turnarounds or Sonny Terry's triplet riffs.

Exercise #24: The Simplified Second Position Blues Riff #1 (Bends: None, Position: 2nd)

Now we'll add rhythm to this scale with the use of eighth notes. These beamed notes are held for half a beat, so if you don't have a lot of rhythm skills yet, practice counting out loud: "One and two three four" for a moment before trying it.

TRACK 24

Exercise #25: The Simplified Second Position Blues Scale Riff #2 (Bends: None, Position: 2nd)

Here's a slightly more complex version of the blues scale, interesting enough to be called a "riff." "Jumping around" (here, from a 4 draw to a 6 blow) on the notes of the blues scale and repeating notes is how we learn to create the note sequences known as riffs, runs, and solos – the last two of which we'll define soon. If this one is difficult for you, practice the simpler versions above for a while.

TRACK 25

Exercise #26: A Fairly Easy IV Chord Riff (Bends: None, Position: 2nd)

If you review Exercise #4 in Week 1 – The 12-Bar Blues Chord Progression – you'll see that, when playing in second position, the most basic chord of bars 5 and 6 are 4-5-6 blow chords. The 4 blow is known as the "root" of this chord and is the most "safe sounding" (although not necessarily the most exciting sounding) note to use during these bars. Here's a simple IV chord riff based on notes from the blues scale to use during this part of the 12-bar. Our IV chord riffs will become much bluesier once we include bent notes (Week 12).

(Until now, all the eighth notes we've encountered have been beamed together with other eighth notes. On beat 4 of the first measure here, you'll notice a single flagged eighth note. The rest that follows – it looks somewhat like the number 7 – is an eighth rest. Like an eighth note, it takes up half-a-beat in 4/4 time.)

TRACK 26

Exercise #27: Turning a Riff into a Turnaround (Bends: None, Position: 2nd)

As stated earlier, second position harmonica turnarounds usually end on either the 1 draw or the 4 draw note (or occasionally the 8 draw), as these are all the same note – the root note of the V chord. By changing a single note of Exercise #25, we create a turnaround that will fit in well with the main riff when we combine some of the above into a 12-bar blues solo.

TRACK 27

Exercise #28: Blues Solo Based on Eighth-Note Riffs (Bends: None, Position: 2nd)

This is just what the title says. If you practiced the above riffs, this solo won't just sound fine – it'll be a snap with just one tiny variation (a long 6 blow) in the second bar. Notice how bars 5 and 6 emphasize the 4 blow note and bars 9 and 10 emphasize the 4 draw and 4 blow, respectively, to shape the solo. A solo of this type can be played along with backing music (other musicians) or entirely by itself; it will still make musical sense, since the soloist is hinting at the chord structure that underlies the solo.

TRACK 28

WEEK 6

This week, we'll learn the standard 12-bar rock chord progression. It's almost the same as the 12-bar blues progression, but is often based on a different rhythm: the "backbeat."

Exercise #29: The Rock One-Bar Backbeat Riff (Bends: None, Position: 2nd)

Most rock music, like most blues music, is broken up into four-beat bars. To play a backbeat, we emphasize the second and fourth beat of each bar. (Notice the accent marks above these 3-4 draw chords.) Rock musicians often break each first and third beat into two equal parts.

TRACK 29

Exercise #30: The Rock Two-Bar Backbeat Riff (Bends: None, Position: 2nd)

This exercise demonstrates a common rhythmic pattern for the second bar of a two-bar rock riff.

TRACK 30

Exercise #31: The Rock Backbeat IV Chord Riff (Bends: None, Position: 2nd)

This two-bar riff maintains the backbeat, but fits better into the bars 5 and 6 of a 12-bar rock chord progression.

TRACK 31

Exercise #32: The Rock Backbeat V–IV Chord Riff (Bends: None, Position: 2nd)

This two-bar riff will work perfectly as the bars 9 and 10 of a 12-bar rock progression. If you're not sure what else to do, you can use it in the same place in most 12-bar blues solos. Start with empty lungs and articulate all the draw chords – daaah DAda dada DAda – before switching to the blow chord.

TRACK 32

Exercise #33: The 12-Bar Rock Solo/Progression (Bends: None, Position: 2nd)

We'll combine the riffs just learned to produce a 12-bar rock solo that follows the 12-bar rock chord progression. The biggest difference between the 12-bar rock and 12-bar blues progression is that, many times, the rock chord progression does not end with a bar of the V chord. Instead, both bars 11 and 12 are I chords.

TRACK 33

Exercise #34: The Rock Backbeat Blues Scale Riff, Going Up (Bends: None, Position: 2nd)

Apply backbeat rhythm to our simplified blues scale and you'll open the door to lots of great rock riffs.

TRACK 34

Exercise #35: The Rock Backbeat Blues Scale Riff, Going Down (Bends: None, Position: 2nd)

TRACK 35

Exercise #36: Fancier 12-Bar Rock Solo/Progression (Bends: None, Position: 2nd)

After you learn the previous two blues-scale rock riffs, try substituting the two-bar "up" riff (Exercise #34) for the first four bars of the previous 12-bar rock solo. The two-bar "down" version (Exercise #35) can be substituted for the last two-bars. Here's what you'd get:

TRACK 36

WEEK 7

This week, we'll tackle more difficult jumps, including the 2 draw to 6 blow, and use them in both a rock solo and a blues solo. A hint for near-beginners: putting the tip of a forefinger just above the 6 hole will help you learn this jump. (Don't do it in front of other musicians, though; it's a newbie giveaway.) Soon the coordination between your hand and mouth will have put all these jump distances into muscle memory. Then just wing it. You'll hit the right hole more often than you might expect.

Exercise #37: The Easy 2 Draw to 6 Blow Jump (Bends: None, Position: 2nd)

The one-beat rests between notes will give you time to find the 2 or 6 hole.

Exercise #38: More 2 Draw to 6 Blow Jump Practice (Bends: None, Position: 2nd)

Try to keep it clean and crisp. If you hit the wrong note, just re-focus and do it again, more slowly.

Exercise #39: The 1 Blow/4 Blow/7 Blow Jumps (Bends: None, Position: 2nd)

If you need to, keep your mouth a bit more open to get two-note chords or even three-note chords. That way, you'll probably hit the right hole at least some of the time. The rests should help as well. The 4 blow and 7 blow (like the 1 blow) are the "root notes" of the IV chord, so they'll always help make bars 5 and 6 of a 12-bar sound "right," especially when playing without backing music.

Exercise #40: The Jumping 12-Bar Blues Solo (Bends: None, Position: 2nd)

Here's a useful jumping exercise. It sounds good as well, played with backing or without.

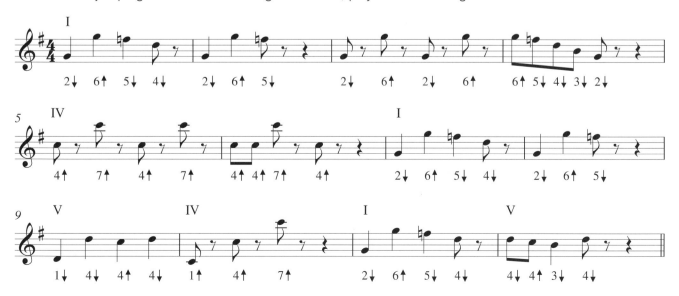

21

Exercise #41: The "Easy" 2 Draw to 6 Blow Backbeat Riff (Bends: None, Position: 2nd)

We'll work on a few jumping rock riffs and then combine them into a solo. This one may prove a challenge, but you'll get it in time. Don't hesitate to go back and practice the 2 draw to 6 blow jump some more if you need to.

TRACK 41

Exercise #42: The "Hard" 2 Draw to 6 Blow Jump Rock Backbeat Riff and Solo (Bends: None, Position: 2nd)

This is a good exercise indeed for practicing and using this hard jump in a real-life riff. Play it twice. Then continue on, using riffs from Week 6, to use it as the main theme of an entire 12-bar rock solo.

TRACK 42

WEEK 8

Exercise #43: The Simplified Second Position Blues Scale Triplet Articulations (Bends: None, Position: 2nd)

In this simple exercise, we introduce the *triplet* eighth-note rhythm (one beat split into three notes) and use the tongue (by whispering "da da da" or "ta ta ta" through the harp) to break each pitch into those three equal pieces. Remember to stay empty during the first rest, since you'll need lots of inhale power for the next triplets.

TRACK 43

Exercise #44: The Simplified Second Position Blues Scale Triplets (Bends: None, Position: 2nd)

Here we see the use of triplet rhythm with different notes. This etude will give you a good 6 blow/5 draw/4 draw workout. You can articulate each note with a "ta" or "da" after you get the hang of doing it without articulation. Articulate at least the first note of each triplet, once you feel ready. This is demonstrated on the audio track.

TRACK 44

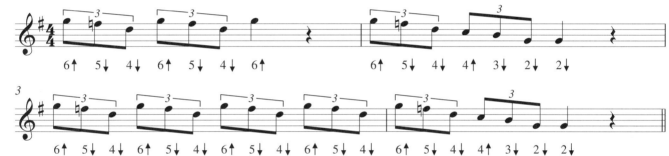

Exercise #45: Another Triplet Blues Scale Riff (Bends: None, Position: 2nd)

Here's another variation on the blues scale – and yes, it's hard. Try it slower.

TRACK 45

Exercise #46: Easy Triplet IV Chord "Sandwich Note" Riff (Bends: None, Position: 2nd)

As you've seen when playing the 12-bar boogie woogie, we can use notes that are not part of the blues scale when playing blues music – as long as we don't use them too often or for too long. In jazz, notes like these are called "passing tones" (because we play them "in passing"), but I prefer to call them "sandwich notes," as we sandwich them in between blues scale notes – as this triplet riff demonstrates. Often, doing something different from what you did during the four bars of the I chord is enough to make your two IV chord bars sound good.

TRACK 46

Exercise #47: Easy Triplet Bridge (V–IV Chord) Riff (Bends: None, Position: 2nd)

This two-bar triplet riff will fit perfectly into bars 9 and 10 of a 12-bar chord structure.

TRACK 47

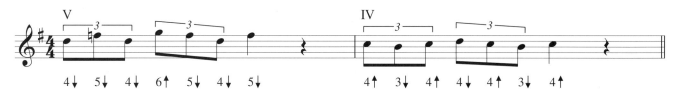

Exercise #48: Moderately Simple Triplet Turnaround (Bends: None, Position: 2nd)

Better practice this one before you try the solo!

TRACK 48

Exercise #49: A Triplet 12-Bar Solo (Bends: None, Position: 2nd)

Most solos have a wider variety of rhythms than this one. It is chock full of triplets, with a few quarter and eighth notes. Since we have not yet covered "swing rhythm" – which is often used with triplets – consider it a good triplet exercise. And it sounds fine when played along with a slow blues accompaniment.

TRACK 49

24

Exercise #50: Glottal Stop (aka "Throat Vibrato") Exercise (Bends: Any, Position: Any)

As described earlier, this tone effect is created by silently articulating the syllable "uh" (as in "Uh-oh!") on either the inhale or exhale. It takes most students months (or years) to perfect. You can begin by doing a triplet "uh-uh-uh" on any particular note. In the example, you'll hear a two-bar throat vibrato riff on the note 4 draw. It can be done on any note or bend, though I rarely use it on a hole higher than 6. It's hard not to make any throat noise (you can even hear Little Walter make some on certain solos), but the sound of the note should be loud enough to mask it. We'll use it in some of the later solos, but it won't be notated. Listen to the demo on the audio track to get a sense of how it should sound.

(Here, a whole note (four beats) is tied to another whole note, for a total of eight beats.)

TRACK 50

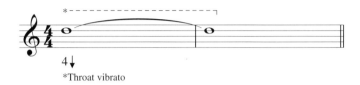

4↓

*Throat vibrato

WEEK 9

Many advanced-beginner, intermediate, and even accomplished harp players regularly (or exclusively) use second position for playing blues and rock. That's not necessarily a good thing. Introducing players to third position blues harp early in their career tends to make their playing – especially their improvising – more creative.

We'll use the Dorian scale, from way back in Week 2, to create a third position blues scale. This style of harmonica tends to produce a wistful, plaintive feel in the listener or the player. It requires single-noting skills. (Second position harmonica is more forgiving if you're not good at single noting yet.) Let's define third position harmonica. Let's say you are using a key of C harmonica. When playing in third position, you will produce music in the key of D or D minor. When playing in second position, you will produce music in the key of G.

Exercise #51: The Easiest (Dorian) Minor Scale (Bends: None, Position: 3rd)

Begin by reviewing this easy, wistful scale from Week 2.

Exercise #52: The Third Position 12-Bar Chord Structure (Bends: None, Position: 3rd)

This is the simplest possible third position 12-bar blues, with one note representing each chord. Here, we're in the key of D minor. Remember that lowercase Roman numerals indicate minor chords.

Exercise #53: The Easiest Third Position Blues Scale, Going Up (Bends: None, Position: 3rd)

Simply by omitting two-notes from the Dorian scale, we produce a third position blues scale. Try it, moving from low to high.

Exercise #54: The Easiest Third Position Blues Scale, Going Down (Bends: None, Position: 3rd)

Now try the same thing, moving from high to low.

26

Exercise #55: The Third Position Blues Scale Jumping Riffs (Bends: None, Position: 3rd)

The most important jump in third position is from the 4 draw to the 8 draw, as these (like the 1 draw) are all the same note an octave or two apart.

TRACK 55

4↓ 8↓ 7↑ 6↓ 6↑ 5↓ 6↑ 6↓ 8↓ 4↓ 5↓ 6↑ 6↓ 6↑ 5↓ 4↓

Exercise #56: The Third Position 12-Bar Rock Solo (Bends: None, Position: 3rd)

This 12-bar rock solo has a different feel from our last rock solo on page 22. Why? Because the last rock solo was in second position and this one is in third. So while it rocks, it also has a more plaintive feel. Notice the use of 4 blow; since it is the same note (octave note) as the 7 blow, it works fine as part of a third position solo. Play this solo amplified at a jam session and people will notice it's new and different.

TRACK 56

4↓ 4↓ 4↑ 4↓ 4↓ 5↓ 4↓ 4↓ 4↑ 4↓ 4↓ 4↑ 4↓ 4↓ 5↓ 4↓ 4↓ 4↑ 4↓

6↑ 6↑ 5↓ 6↑ 6↑ 6↓ 6↑ 5↓ 4↓ 4↑ 4↓ 4↓ 4↑ 4↓ 4↓ 5↓ 6↓ 6↑ 5↓ 4↓

6↓ 6↓ 6↓ 6↓ 6↑ 6↓ 6↑ 6↑ 5↓ 6↑ 4↓ 4↓ 4↑ 4↓ 4↓ 5↓ 6↓ 6↑ 5↓ 4↓

Exercise #57: The Third Position Four-Bar Blues Solo (Bends: None, Position: 3rd)

This short etude would work well as the first four bars (the i chord) of a slow minor blues. This four-bar lick would also work well for bars 5-8 of a 12-bar solo: the iv chord in bars 5-6, then back to the i chord for bars 7-8.

TRACK 57

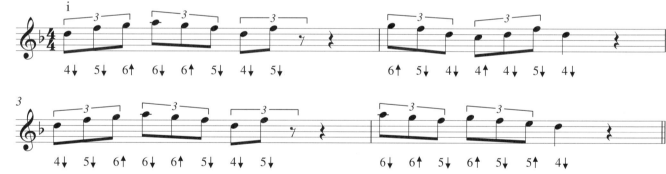

4↓ 5↓ 6↑ 6↓ 6↑ 5↓ 4↓ 5↓ 6↑ 5↓ 4↓ 4↑ 4↓ 5↓ 4↓

4↓ 5↓ 6↑ 6↓ 6↑ 5↓ 4↓ 5↓ 6↓ 6↑ 5↓ 6↑ 5↓ 5↑ 4↓

Exercise #58: The Third Position Four-Bar Blues Turnaround (Bends: None, Position: 3rd)

Simply by changing the last few notes, we create a turnaround that makes a good four-bar introduction to a slow blues or is effective as the last four bars of a 12-bar blues. Playing Exercise #57 twice, then playing Exercise #58, will produce a simple but satisfying 12-bar, third position blues solo (audio example 58B).

TRACK 58

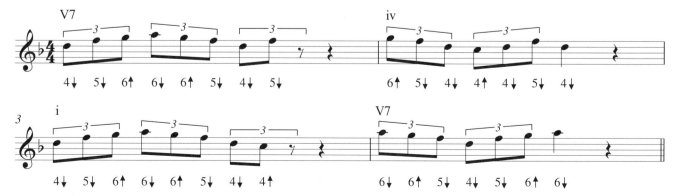

4↓ 5↓ 6↑ 6↓ 6↑ 5↓ 4↓ 5↓ 6↑ 5↓ 4↓ 4↑ 4↓ 5↓ 4↓

4↓ 5↓ 6↑ 6↓ 6↑ 5↓ 4↓ 4↑ 6↓ 6↑ 5↓ 4↓ 5↓ 6↑ 6↓

So far we've used mostly single beats, half beats, and triplet beats in our riffs and solos. A lot of blues music, and some rock, uses "shuffle" or "swing" rhythms. Basically, these involve breaking a single beat into two unequal parts: approximately two-thirds of a beat and one-third of a beat.

The most common way to indicate swing rhythms in musical notation is to write the words "swing," "swing eighths," "shuffle feel," or something similar at the beginning. This tells you that, whenever you see eighth notes, you should play each set of two so that the first one is longer than the second. Sometimes composers and arrangers include a little diagram that tells you the same thing:

Going forward, we'll use the symbol above to refer to this timing. After a few practice exercises using swung eighth notes with single beats, we'll start applying this new rhythm to a variety of riffs and solos. Listen to the audio track examples and you'll get it.

Exercise #59: Easy Swing Chord Practice (Bends: None, Position: 2nd)

No single notes, no tough note combinations – just swing it. Use the tip of your tongue to articulate a rhythm like this: Daaa da Daaa da Daah!

TRACK 59

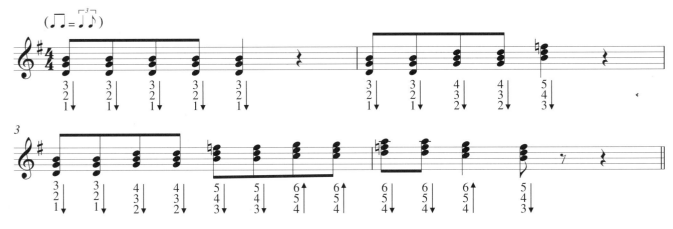

Exercise #60: Swinging Train Rhythm (Bends: None, Position: 2nd)

Once you've got this train down well and can do it at various speeds, we'll use it as the basis for a train solo you can expand upon whenever you learn new second position riffs. You can play the third beat of each bar as either a 1-2 draw chord or a single 1 draw note, or alternate between them. Practice this with a metronome so you can slow or speed your train solo at will.

TRACK 60

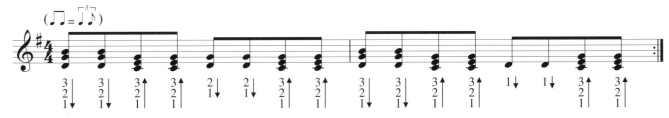

Exercise #61: Swinging Train Solo (Bends: None, Position: 2nd)

Repeat the basic train rhythm for as long as you want. When you're ready to add some riffs (the "whistles"), use bar 4 below, which both helps set off your riffs and gives you one beat of rest to get ready for them. Then add some riffs – perhaps some you've learned earlier in the book – or the simplified blues scale examples here; then return to the basic train. After some more train, slow it down and throw in a triplet riff as a whistle. (Triplets fit in nicely with swing rhythms.) Once you've got the feel of it, make up a train solo of your own.

TRACK 61

Move back to the basic train and pre-riff whistle train. (Slow it down; the next whistle is hard and contains triplets.)

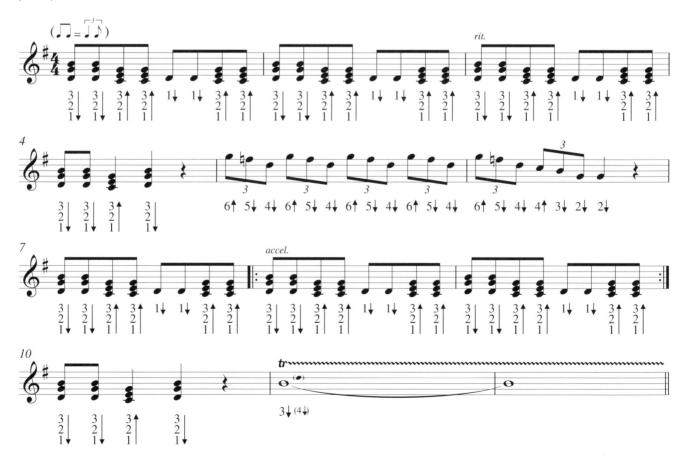

Then move back to the basic train, and so on. In Week 11, we'll learn a slightly fancier basic swinging train variation.

This week, we'll continue our study of swing, starting with a classic 12-bar blues pattern that will allow you to take on the duties of the rhythm guitarist or bass player for a few verses. This specific 12-bar is called the "shuffle." (That's one reason we'll use "swing" rather than shuffle to refer to the two-thirds:one-third ratio beat pattern.) You can hear it as the background of countless blues songs. We'll also fancy up our swinging train and play some riffs with a mix of swing and triplet timing.

Exercise #62: Swinging Blues Shuffle (Bends: None, Position: 2nd)

People sometimes play this with an exaggerated swing feel so that the first note of every set of eighth notes is more than twice as long as the second note. Do what feels right to you – unless you're playing along with other musicians, then do it like the bass player does it.

TRACK 62

Exercise #63: Fancier Basic Swinging Train (Bends: None, Position: 2nd)

While you're working on your swing, here's a favorite variation on the swing rhythm train. It will sound even better when you add a touch of bending to the 3 in note, which we'll cover in Week 12. Replace any two bars of your train with this new version.

TRACK 63

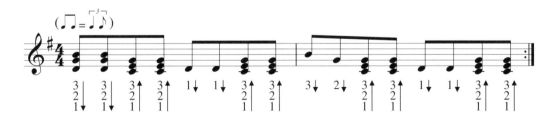

Exercise #64: Swing and Triplet Practice (Bends: None, Position: 2nd)

If rhythm is not your strong point, alternating swing beats and triplets in this exercise will help you with the following 12-bar solo.

TRACK 64

Exercise #65: Swing and Triplet Blues 12-Bar Solo (Bends: None, Position: 2nd)

Although it uses the simplified version of the blues scale, this solo will sound good played by itself or along with almost any tempo of 12-bar blues backing music you're comfortable with.

TRACK 65

If you can't bend notes *at all*, you can work on this essential blues and rock harp technique while you skip to some of the later weeks that don't require bending. (See, for example, the "Country Pentatonic Scale" in Week 18 or the "High End Blues Scale" in Week 20.) This week will focus on the use of short draw partial bends on two-note chords that release almost instantly to the unbent note, represented in the notation by small "grace notes" with lines through the stem. For most, these are the easiest bends to play.

Note: The bend on the 5 draw note is closer to a quarter step than a half step. In other words, it's in between the F and E keys on a piano; for simplicity's sake, it's been written throughout the book as a half-step bend in both the notation and the tab.

Exercise #66: 3-4 Draw Partial Bend Practice (Bends: 3-4 partial, Position: 2nd)

Practice a partial bend on the two-hole 3-4 draw chord, then use it in place of the 3 draw. Hit the grace notes 3-4 draw slightly bent, just before the beat. Release the tongue tension that creates the slight bend exactly as the beat falls. Listen to the audio example if this seems confusing.

TRACK 66

Exercise #67: 4-5 in Partial Bend Practice (Bends: 4-5 partial, Position: 2nd)

Now do the same on the two-hole 4-5 draw chord. A word to those beginning to bend notes: Whenever you change which notes you are trying to bend, the tongue position you need to use also changes; that's what makes bending so difficult to learn without help.

TRACK 67

Exercise #68: Almost Real Second Position Blues Scale, Ascending (Bends: 3-4 and 4-5 partial, Position: 2nd)

Add your two new partial bend chords to the blues scale. It sounds much bluesier! Practice going carefully and accurately from the single note 2 draw to the 3-4 draw partial bend and from the 4-5 draw partial bend to the single 5 draw.

TRACK 68

Exercise #69: Almost Real Second Position Blues Scale, Descending (Bends: 3-4 and 4-5 partial, Position: 2nd)

Moving from 6 blow to 2 draw, do the same thing. Practice going carefully and accurately from the single notes to the partial bends.

TRACK 69

Exercise #70: Two-Bar Partial Bend Riff #1 (Bends: 3-4 and 4-5 partial, Position: 2nd)

Let's add partial bends to the first three exercises in Week 3. This will make them sound much more interesting. It will also be easy, since we already know how to play these riffs without grace-note bends.

Exercise #71: Two-Bar IV Chord Partial Bend Riff #1 (Bends: 4-5 partial, Position: 2nd)

We can treat the following riff from Week 3 similarly. In this case, the grace-note bends fall in the middle of the riff and turn a not-very-bluesy riff into a better-sounding one.

Exercise #72: Two-Bar IV Chord Partial Bend Riff #2 (Bends: 3-4 partial, Position: 2nd)

In this variation of Exercise #70 above, we'll use only the 3-4 partial bend.

Exercise #73: The 5-6 Draw Partial Bend Practice (Bends: 5-6 partial, Position: 2nd)

Add a grace-note bend to the 5-6 draw chord. The tongue position required to create this bend will be slightly different from the tongue motion that produces the 3-4 draw and 4-5 draw partial bends. But if you can do them, you'll figure this one out.

Exercise #74: Two-Bar V–IV Chord Partial Bend Riff
(Bends: 5-6 and 4-5 partial, Position: 2nd)

Now we'll use the 5-6 draw partial bend in a V–IV chord combination – i.e., as the "bridge" of a 12-bar progression.

Exercise #75: Two-Bar Partial Bend Turnaround Riff (Bends: 3-4 partial, Position: 2nd)

Keeping the theme of our solo consistent, let's go down to the 1 draw to finish our 12-bar solo with a turnaround.

We'll begin this week with a solo based on the riffs from last week and then work on ways to use partial bends in our trains. We'll also practice "skeleton blues." These are 12-bar blues progressions in which we, as harp players, simply help the progression along with "fills" that imply chord changes. Bands like blues harpists who can do this (and who don't feel compelled to play a solo in each verse, or else to sit out).

Exercise #76: Partial Bend 12-Bar Blues Solo (Bends: 3-4, 4-5, and 5-6 partial, Position: 2nd)

We'll start out with something easy. If you've practiced last week's exercises, this solo will be a snap, since all we have to do is play the riffs in the right order. By now, you can begin to identify the chord changes in any standard 12-bar blues you listen to.

TRACK 76

Exercise #77: Preparation for the 12-Bar "Skeleton Blues"
(Bends: 3-4 partial, Position: 2nd)

This exercise will help you get ready for the next one. Although the timing of the rests is different, and the order of the two-beat partial bend-to-unbent note (or chord) riffs is different, the riffs themselves are the same. Notice that this is a stretched-out and more interesting version of Exercise #2: The Two-Bar, Three-Chord Rock Chord Progression, from way back in Week 1.

TRACK 77

Exercise #78: 12-Bar "Skeleton Blues" (Bends: 3-4 partial, Position: 2nd)

Why is this a "skeleton?" Because we provide only the bare bones of the 12-bar progression, leaving space for other instrumentalists to shine. This is also a great exercise to practice with just the metronome, as it will help you burn the 12-bar progression into your brain. You'll begin this after a count of three (not four), hitting the first 2 draw exactly as the 12-bar begins. (This note that begins before the first bar is called a *pickup note*.) After 14 (Count 'em off!) beats of silence, you'll play your 3-4 draw bend just before moving to the IV chord, with your 4-5 blow as the first note of the new chord, and so on. Listen to the audio – many times, if necessary – if you find this explanation confusing. It's easier to hear and play than to read about.

Exercise #79: Multiple Partial Bend Practice (Bends: 3-4, 4-5, and 5-6 partial, Position: 2nd)

This three-bar exercise will help you play multiple partial bend chords – three in a row, with one beat apiece. Try to make each one clear.

Exercise #80: Adding a Trill to a Partial Bend (Bends: 3-4, 4-5, and 5-6 partial, Position: 2nd)

Going directly from a partial bend on a two-note chord to a trill on that same chord is a classic harmonica effect. Once you can do it smoothly, you'll find lots of places to use it.

Exercise #81: The Swinging Train with Multiple Partial Bends and Trills
(Bends: 3-4, 4-5, and 5-6 partial, Position: 2nd)

Once you've practiced this exercise, make up some similar trains of your own. As the train goes faster, use a higher-pitched whistle to add excitement. Remember to vary the volume of the train to reflect whether it's coming toward you or going away from you. (If you're on the train, the volume stays the same, although the whistles are always louder than the wheel rhythms.)

WEEK 14

Now that we're accustomed to using partial bends on the 3-4, 4-5, and 5-6 draw chords, it's time to make our second position rock riffs sound bluesier. Our IV chord riffs especially have had a lightweight sound since, when playing in second position ("cross harp"), we need to bend the 3 draw to get the correct note of the blues scale. The unbent 3 or 3-4 draw notes do not sound that great. (This is one reason most of our riffs so far don't hold those notes very long.) Substituting the 3-4 draw partial bend will work much better. After practicing the new IV chord part and a new V–VI bridge, we'll use them in a rock solo.

Exercise #82: Rock IV Chord Practice with Partial Bends
(Bends: 3-4 partial, Position: 2nd)

Practice going accurately from 4 blow to the partial-bend chords. The first line has simpler timing, but the second will sound livelier. Use whichever you prefer in the solo.

Exercise #83: New Rock V–IV Riff with Partial Bends
(Bends: 3-4 and 4-5 partial, Position: 2nd)

This exercise looks complicated in notation, but if you've practiced playing multiple partial bends, you can do it.

Exercise #84: 12-Bar Rock Solo with Partial Bends (Bends: 3-4 and 4-5, Position: 2nd)

Adding the 3-4 draw partial bend will improve the tone of our basic I chord rock riff, but not as much as it will improve the tone of our IV chord riffs. This exercise is not swung – each of the eighth notes is played for the same length of time. In measure 4, we contract the last two notes into a single beat. Use whichever version of the above IV chord riff you prefer. (The solo that follows uses the harder one).

Exercise #85: Rock Riff Variations (Bends: 3-4 and 4-5 partial, Position: 2nd)

You can create new rock 12-bars by learning variations on the basic I chord riff and using them along with the IV chord and V–VI chord riffs you already know. For example, try substituting this four-bar variation for the first four bars of the previous solo.

This week, we'll practice sliding and partial bends, followed by the 4-5 partial bend to 6 blow jump. Then we'll work on using similar riffs and techniques in a new solo: the classic folk-blues-rock song, "The House of the Rising Sun" (sometimes known as "Rising Sun Blues"). Later on, we'll learn versions of this song in different positions using more challenging bends.

Exercise #86: Sliding Practice #1 (Bends: 3-4 partial, Position: 2nd)

Make sure your lips are wet, and we'll practice some draw sliding (mostly used in second position). We'll use 5 blow notes in this exercise to get ready for the "Country Pentatonic Scale" in Week 18. Swing the eighth notes, as per the little symbol above the bold 4/4 time signature. The last slide is notated with a "draw slide" between the 5 draw and 1 draw, so hold the 5 draw for almost a whole beat and then swiftly slide down to hit the 1 draw on the next beat. Don't worry about the super-fast triplet too much; just hit that 1 draw note as your foot taps the floor. This four-bar riff would make a good intro to a slow 12-bar blues.

Exercise #87: Sliding Practice #2 (Bends: 4-5 and 5-6 partial, Position: 2nd)

Now we'll practice sliding down to the 1 draw from a partial bend, a technique that will be invaluable for turnarounds (the last bar or two of a 12-bar blues). Don't obsess over the timing of the slide; just hit the 1 draw right on the beat. This will become easy with a bit of practice.

Exercise #88: A Good Sliding Turnaround Bar (Bends: 4-5 partial, Position: 2nd)

We can create a great variety of turnarounds by learning this bar and then preceding it with variations, as we'll soon see in Exercise #89.

Exercise #89: Two-Bar Bend and Slide Turnaround #1 (Bends: 4-5 partial, Position: 2nd)

By twice repeating a slight timing variation of the first two beats of the previous exercise, followed by the entire bar, we create a two-bar turnaround that has a "thematic" feel – the theme being a slide downward from the 4-5 draw partial bend.

TRACK 89

Exercise #90: 4-5 Partial Bend to 6 Blow Jump Practice
(Bends: 4-5 partial, Position: 2nd)

This jump sounds great, so let's practice it for later use in a 12-bar blues solo.

TRACK 90

Exercise #91: House of the Rising Sun (Bends: 3-4 and 4-5 partial, Position: 2nd)

This might not be the most exciting harp solo ever played for the song, but your listeners will recognize and enjoy it. The following will sound just fine when played either alone or with backing in the right key for second position. (In this case, we're using a key of C harmonica with backing music in the key of G minor.) The song starts after the guitar introduction on an upbeat, with the first note as the last third of a triplet.

TRACK 91

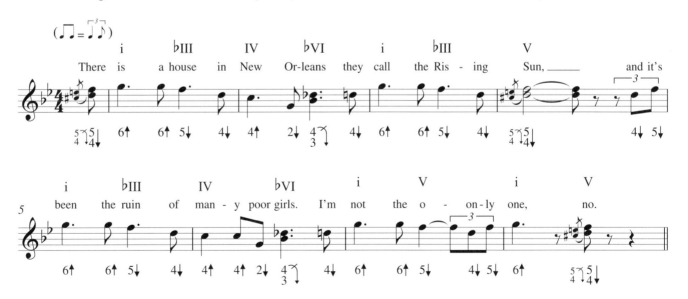

This week, we'll begin using simple single-note bends in second and third position riffs and solos. If you're not yet able to bend the 4, 5, and 6 draw notes, start working hard on that. While you do so, scan the exercises for the next few weeks, some of which don't require single-note bending. If you can already bend the 1 draw of your key of C harp, you can do Week 17 first.

Exercise #92: Quick Release Bends (QRBs) on Single Notes (Bends: QRBs 4, 5, and 6, Position: 3rd)

Hitting a single bent note and then releasing it quickly is the first step in being able to maintain a bend. Let's begin with that. Get your mouth centered on the single note and go for it. The simple rhythm here, with a whole beat to get ready for the next note, should make this easier.

Exercise #93: Staccato QRBs on Single Notes (Bends: QRBs 4, 5, and 6, Position: 3rd)

In this exercise, play the grace notes (partial bends) in staccato style – i.e., crisply. *Staccato* notes are indicated by a dot over the note. We make a bend begin in staccato style by beginning the partial bend with a "d" or "t" tongue position, with the tongue blocking all air by pressing up behind the upper front teeth; then we retract the tongue to the proper bend position. The 5 draw bend is not *really* a full half step, though it is notated that way. And playing QRBs on 5 draw sound great, full bend or not.

Exercise #94: Staccato QRB Solo (Bends: QRBs 4, 5, and 6, Position: 3rd)

Third position is probably the easiest position to practice our staccato QRBs, as three of the most important mid-range blues scale notes in that position are 4, 5, and 6 draw. If the timing on this minor blues solo seems challenging, listen to it several times. If you make some of your own slight variations, just call it improvisation.

Exercise #95: Staccato QBR Boogie Woogie 12-Bar
(Bends: QRBs 3, 4, 5 and 6, Position: 2nd)

In addition to our previous third position solo, let's practice a swinging solo in second position. We'll add a staccato QRB to our 3 draw note as well. The 3 draw can be bent to produce three separate distinct notes, so don't overdo it.

TRACK 95

WEEK 17

Some students find all aspects of single-note bending – bending a note down, holding it bent, starting it bent – easier on 1 draw than on 4, 5, or 6 draw. This is partly because it's easier to get 1 draw as a single note (there's no 0 hole) and partly because the tongue motion required to bend 1 draw is a larger movement and less subtle. Also, unlike most other bends, the 1 draw bend cannot be "overbent" (bent too far down). So this week, we'll play riffs and a solo that add this useful bent note.

Exercise #96: 1 Draw Bend Practice #1 (Bends: 1, Position: 2nd)

Make sure you can hit the 1 draw note and then bend it down, crisply and accurately.

TRACK 96

Exercise #97: 1 Draw Bend Practice #2 (Bends: 1, Position: 2nd)

Now we'll articulate everything for a crisper feel. To that end, start each note, bent or not, with an articulation. We'll also add a 1 blow note for reasons you'll soon understand.

TRACK 97

Exercise #98: Hitting the 1 Draw Bent Practice (Bends: 1, Position: 2nd)

Hitting the 1 draw note bent provides a riff we'll use to create a new second position blues scale. The first two 1 draw bends are played staccato.

TRACK 98

Exercise #99: An Easy 1 Draw Bent Riff (Bends: 1, Position: 2nd)

Adding a 1 blow note after and before a 1 draw bend makes the bend a bit harder, but it's good practice.

TRACK 99

Exercise #100: Near-Blues Scale with 1 Draw Bend #1
(Bends: 1; and 3 partial, Position: 2nd)

Though we have not yet worked with the other three bends – full 2 draw, partial 3 draw, and partial 4 draw – needed to play a complete low-end second position blues scale, we can "jump down" and substitute our 1 draw bend for the missing 4 draw bend and play a riff based on this blues scale "down low." It's not an authentic blues scale, but it sounds good. (The penultimate note is wrong: it should be a 2 draw full bend.)

TRACK 100

Exercise #101: Near-Blues Scale with 1 Draw Bend #2
(Bends: 1; and 3 partial, Position: 2nd)

This is a bona fide blues scale. It requires either a jump or a slide from 5 draw to 1 draw to avoid a more difficult 2 draw bend. (We'll practice the latter in Week 22.)

TRACK 101

Exercise #102: 1 Draw Bend 12-Bar Blues Solo
(Bends: 1; and 3, 3-4, and 5 partial, Position: 2nd)

There are lots of 1 draw bends in this solo. It's meant to be played with a slow blues backing, so it may not sound great if played without it – unless you have that 12-bar blues embedded in your mind. Listen to the audio track a few times and then try it. Feel free to add your own touches: play with the rhythm, add extra trills or QRBs, hold the long 1 draw bends down, and wah-wah them without mercy!

TRACK 102

Note: If you are working on bending but cannot reliably use 4, 5, and 6 draw bends, continue practicing those while working through the following "non-bending" weeks. They'll provide lots of satisfying music without much extra work. If you can bend the 4, 5, and 6 draw notes pretty well, you can go straight to Week 24 and return to Weeks 18–23 whenever your tongue needs a break.

WEEK 18

The last few weeks have had some technically difficult material. So this week, we'll learn the country pentatonic scale. It's easy to play if you fudge one bend, without which it still sounds okay, but will provide a new way of creating a variety of improvised music in genres ranging from blues to rock to country. In fact, the simplified ascending scale in Exercise #103 is used to provide one of the most famous verses in blues history.

Exercise #103: The Easy Country Pentatonic Scale, Going Up (Bends: QRB 3, Position: 2nd)

In this simplified version, we'll hit the 3 draw note with a QRB instead of holding it partly bent; it will still sound fine. Fans of the amazing blues harpist Little Walter will notice that the first verse of his best-known song "Juke" is composed of just this scale, with slightly fancier rhythms and an extra 6 blow note.

TRACK 103

Exercise #104: The Easy Country Pentatonic Scale, Going Down (Bends: QRB 3, Position: 2nd)

This is the same thing going down. This one doesn't work quite as well as the uphill version, but we'll fix that in a minute.

TRACK 104

Exercise #105: The Easy Extended Country Pentatonic Scale, Going Up (Bends: QRB 3, Position: 2nd)

By adding the octave notes 1 draw (same note as 4 draw an octave lower) and 2 blow (same as 5 blow an octave lower), we can use even this easy version to create great-sounding riffs that will work in a variety of musical genres.

TRACK 105

Exercise #106: The Easy Extended Country Pentatonic Scale, Going Down (Bends: QRB 3, Position: 2nd)

This is the same as above, but with the direction reversed.

TRACK 106

Exercise #107: Easy Extended Country Pentatonic Scale Up/Down Riff
(Bends: QRB 3, Position: 2nd)

If you've practiced the last two exercises, this one will be easy. It just adds some rhythm and a jump.

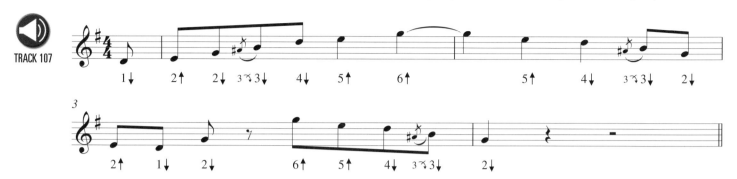

Exercise #108: The Easy Eight-Bar Country Pentatonic Solo
(Bends: QRB 3 and 4, Position: 2nd)

This chord structure is used in songs as varied as the country folk classic "The Wreck of the Old 97" and the main verses of the Rolling Stone's "Country Honk." You might want to review its most basic form (Week 1) before playing the solo. If you do, you'll see why the solo emphasizes the 4 blow note during certain parts (the IV chord sections) to help shape the solo.

WEEK 19

The four-bar rock ballad chord structure was used in lots of rock music of the early 1960s, perhaps best exemplified by Gene Chandler's oft-imitated No. 1 hit "Duke of Earl." In some ways, it's slightly more structurally complex than the chord progressions we've used so far. In addition to using the I, IV, and V chords, it adds a vi (minor six) chord in its second bar. Progressions aside, simple versions are easy to play if you can articulate single notes. Add some grace-note bends and it sounds great.

Exercise #109: Simplest Four-Bar Rock Ballad Chord Structure (Bends: None, Position: 2nd)

Even played at its simplest with single notes, this is fun, and people who love the music of the 1960s won't be able to help smiling. This example is set in G major.

Exercise #110: Four-Bar Rock Ballad Solo #1 (Bends: None, Position: 2nd)

Ask the band to play a four-bar I–vi–IV–V (one, six, four, five) chord structure in G major. Play this and the following solo (Exercise #111) slowly and soulfully, and the dance floor will fill with vintage rock lovers.

Exercise #111: Four-Bar Rock Ballad Solo #2 (Bends: QRB 3, Position: 2nd)

The rhythms are a bit fancier (swing the eighth notes in the first bar), and we add a few QRBs in this solo. Use triplet hand wahs for each of the first two beats of the last note, with a single, heartfelt wah on the third beat. It's easier than it looks, especially if you play some of the G notes using 3 blow instead of the usual 2 draw. (They're the same note.)

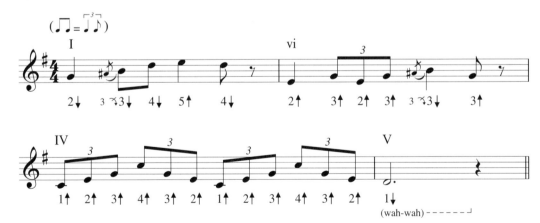

46

Exercise #112: The Simplified Fifth Position Blues Scale (Bends: None, Position: 5th)

When composing or improvising a solo based on a chord structure, a certain position of blues scale will sometimes fit in perfectly with one of the chords of that structure. For example, when playing the second bar of a four-bar rock ballad, the fifth position blues scale falls under this improvising strategy. Look at the first of these two simplified fifth position blues scales below, then look at the second bar of the solo. You'll see what I mean.

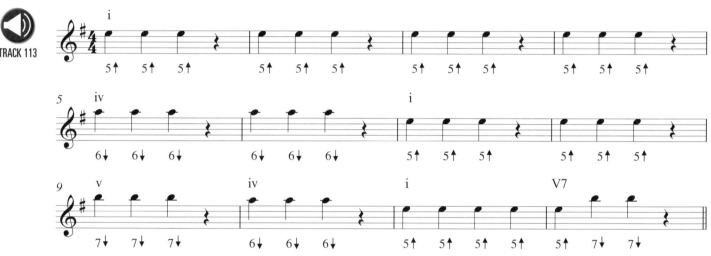

Exercise #113: The Fifth Position 12-Bar Blues (Bends: None, Position: 5th)

Later, we'll go deeper into fifth position playing. But in case you're interested, here is the simplest fifth position 12-bar blues. When played with a C harmonica, this blues will be in the key of E minor.

Exercise #114: Four-Bar Rock Ballad Solo #3 (Bends: QRBs 3 and 6, Position: 2nd)

The country pentatonic scale works perfectly with this chord structure, so let's use it. If you have not practiced that scale, please go back to Week 18 and work on it.

Because your 10-hole blues harmonica includes three octaves' worth of notes, most scales can be played in at least two – and sometimes three – different places: high, middle, and low. So now it's time to learn a simplified high-end version of the second position blues scale. Then we'll combine the high and low blues scales to create "runs," extended riffs that cover a wide range of notes.

Many of my students are good harp players who never learned to use the high end of the harmonica as much as they use holes 1 through 6, so using the high notes is a great habit to develop early on. If the plethora of extra ledger lines above the music staff seems confusing, look at the tablature notation below the staff.

Exercise #115: The Simplified High-End Blues Scale, Going Up (Bends: None, Position: 2nd)

Try this simplified version of the second position blues scale, played from holes 6 through 9.

Exercise #116: The Easy High-End Simplified Blues Scale, Going Down (Bends: None, Position: 2nd)

Now play the same thing going from high to low. Use crisp, clear, single notes and get ready to do it faster.

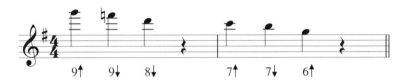

Exercise #117: The Simplified Low and High Blues Scales, Going Up (Bends: None, Position: 2nd)

Put both of these simplified blues scales together, from low to high, and practice them.

Exercise #118: The Simplified High and Low Blues Scales, Going Down (Bends: None, Position: 2nd)

Now do the same thing going from high to low.

Exercise #119: Up & Down High-End Simplified Blues Scale (Bends: None, Position: 2nd)

Play the high-octave blues scale, going from low to high and back again. Use crisp, clear, single notes, and get ready to do it in a triplet rhythm without rests.

Exercise #120: Classic High-End Simplified Blues Riff (Bends: None, Position: 2nd)

This riff is similar to the type of high-end riff often used by the great Blues Traveler harpist John Popper. Of course, we won't do our 9 blow/9 draw/8 draw triplets nearly as fast as he does. (No one can!)

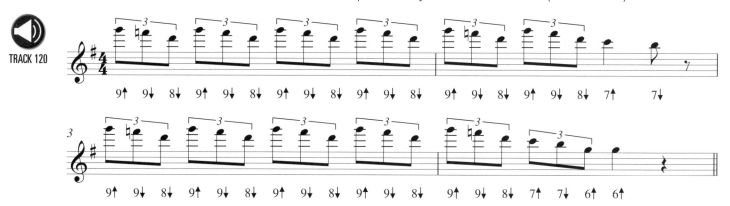

Exercise #121: Low- to High- to Low-End "Run" #1 (Bends: None, Position: 2nd)

A "run" is a term used by many blues, rock, and jazz musicians to refer to a riff (combination of notes) that starts low and ends high, or vice versa. I don't know the origin of the term, but it may be that this kind of riff "runs" a long way.

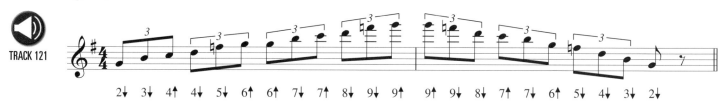

Exercise #122: High- to Low-End "Run" #2 (Bends: QRBs 3-4 and 4-5, Position: 2nd)

This etude adds a few QRBs to make it more interesting.

Exercise #123: High- to Low-End Turnaround Riff (Bends: QRB 4-5, Position: 2nd)

Change the last bar around to create a "turnaround run" riff for a good end to a 12-bar blues.

Exercise #124: High-to-Low Run as a Song Ending
(Bends: QRBs 3, 4 and 4-5, Position: 2nd)

Add a long 45 draw trill that fades out at the end of run #2 to end an entire song, like this.

When playing along with a slow blues background, you can play any 10 bars' worth of the above riffs or exercises and end the 12-bar verse with the turnaround riff from Exercise #123.

49

WEEK 21

Octave blocking (or tongue blocking) is a harmonica tone technique in which we cover four holes with our mouth and block the two middle holes with the tip of our tongue. For example, we might cover holes 1-4 with our mouth and block holes 2 and 3 with the tongue, so that only holes 1 and 4 play. This two-note chord technique is most often used with holes 1 and 4, 2 and 5, 3 and 6, and sometimes 4 and 7 (all on both inhales and exhales).

This provides a great way of adding excitement to your riffs and solos with the contrast between the tone of the octave blocks and the tone of the single notes and bent notes. Octave blocks are most often used in first, second, and third position playing.

Exercise #125: Easy Octave-Block Practice #1 (Bends: None, Position: 3rd)

Listen to this example on the audio track. In practicing, make sure both the 1 and 4 notes are playing simultaneously. It may take some work, especially if you are used to puckering to get single notes.

TRACK 125

Exercise #126: Easy Third Position Octave-Block Riff (Bends: None, Position: 3rd)

Start with your lungs empty and your mouth and tongue on the 1-4 draw. In bars 2 and 4, there's an eighth rest and a quarter rest, so you can jump more easily to the single-note 5 draw and 6 draw, respectively. Be ready to jump back to the 1-4 draw. Play this as many times as you need. The eventual goal is to be able to jump from a single note to an octave block, or vice versa, without the silent beat or half beat. Please disregard the QRBs 5 and 6 on the audio; we'll add those a bit later.

TRACK 126

Exercise #127: Easy Octave-Block Practice #2 (Bends: None, Position: 3rd)

Keep your mouth and tongue in the octave-block position as you move from holes 1-4 to 2-5 to 3-6. Notice, from the standard notation, that the 2-5 and 3-6 draw octave blocks are not really an octave, but instead a I–♭VII (one, flat-seven) jump. It works fine anyway.

TRACK 127

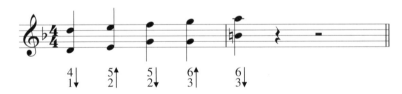

Exercise #128: Super-Easy Octave-Blocking Third Position 12-Bar Blues
(Bends: None, Position: 3rd)

Practicing this will both improve your octave-blocking skills and prepare you for more complicated octave-blocking 12-bars that use bends and harder single-note riffs. When repeating the same octave block (as in bar 3) you'll have to take successive short, sharp breaths to form each two-note chord.

Exercise #129: Octave-Blocking Third Position 12-Bar Blues with Riffs
(Bends: QRBs 5 and 6, Position: 3rd)

Now we'll add some single-note riffs with QRBs between the tongue-blocked chords. This will help you jump from an octave block to any particular single note.

Exercise #130: Octave-Blocking Second Position Practice Riff (Bends: None, Position: 2nd)

Eventually, you'll want to alternate more rapidly between octave blocks, single notes, and bends. If you've mastered the above exercises, riffs, and solos, that won't be too hard. This exercise will help prepare you.

This week, we'll learn the 32-bar AABA jazz chord progression and a few simple solos. However, to play even this relatively easy form of jazz, we'll need to learn a little more about sixth and fourth positions – in addition to the second, third, and fifth positions we've already covered to at least some extent. We'll do that in Week 23.

Exercise #131: The 32-Bar AABA Jazz Chord Structure (Bends: None, Position: 2nd)

There are many variations of this chord progression, sometimes referred to as "Rhythm Changes" because it follows the chord changes of the famous Gershwin classic, "I Got Rhythm." The following version is the simplest. Each verse has three main parts (the "A" parts) and one bridge (the "B" part). Each section is eight bars long, so one entire AABA verse is 32 bars long. This is technically easy, but it's more complex than anything we've done in terms of music theory and chord progressions. Notice that you need to repeat the first eight bars twice, for the AA of the AABA. And, for this simple verse, the last eight bars are exactly the same as the first eight bars.

TRACK 131

Exercise #132: More Interesting Eight-Bar "A" Part #1
(Bends: QRBs 2, 3, 3-4 and 4, Position: 2nd)

This A part follows the same chord progression as the A parts in the previous exercise, but adds more interesting rhythms and a few QRBs. (Practice the QRB 2 draw before you try the whole thing.) If you think about it, it's exactly what we've done with other chord progressions. Practice the simplest version, then fancy it up. Once you learn it, substitute it for the second A part (the repeat of the first eight bars in the last exercise) to add interest to the entire verse.

TRACK 132

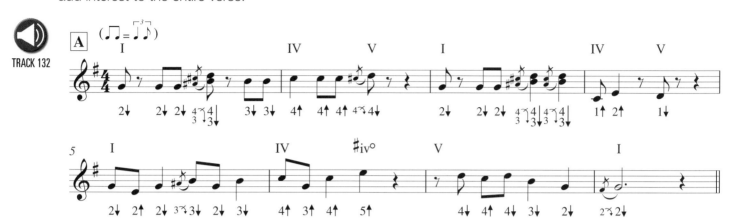

Exercise #133: More Interesting Eight-Bar "A" Part #2
(Bends: QRBs 2, 3, 3-4 and 4, Position: 2nd)

Here's another A part to substitute for any of the A parts in the chord progression above. Try this: Play the easiest A part from the chord progression exercise first, then play A Part #1 above. Continue by playing the simplest B part from the chord progression, followed by the new A part below.

TRACK 133

In second and third positions, you can use QRBs and still play good blues and rock solos. But unless you're good at bending notes, it's hard to play an entire 12-bar blues or rock verse using first, fourth, fifth, or sixth positions. However, you can use those positions for a bar or two, as we did with fifth position in Week 19 (Exercise #112), when playing four-bar rock ballads. This week, we'll learn just enough about these trickier positions (fourth, fifth, and sixth) to use them in the B part of a 32-bar jazz solo; it will sound a lot more interesting than the one-note versions we used last week. Doing this will prepare us for using those positions later on, should we choose to do so – or find ourselves at a jam session with only a few harps and the desire to play in as many keys as possible on each one.

Exercise #134: Fifth Position Scale and 12-Bar Review (Bends: None, Position: 5th)

Let's review the simplified (bend-free) fifth position blues scale and the simplest fifth position 12-bar blues. Using your C harp will produce this scale and 12-bar in the key of E minor.

TRACK 134A

TRACK 134B

Exercise #135: Fourth Position Simplified Blues Scale and 12-Bar (Bends: None, Position: 4th)

This is the same as above, but for fourth position. Using your C harp will produce this scale and 12-bar in the keys of A major and A minor. If you can reliably bend your 3 draw down two half steps (or one whole step), you can play this in the low holes as well. Otherwise, you'll have to jump around, as in the first two bars, or go up high, as in the last two bars.

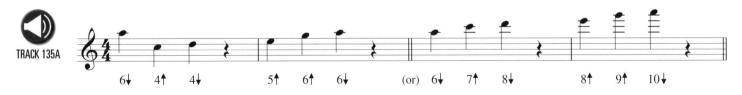

TRACK 135A

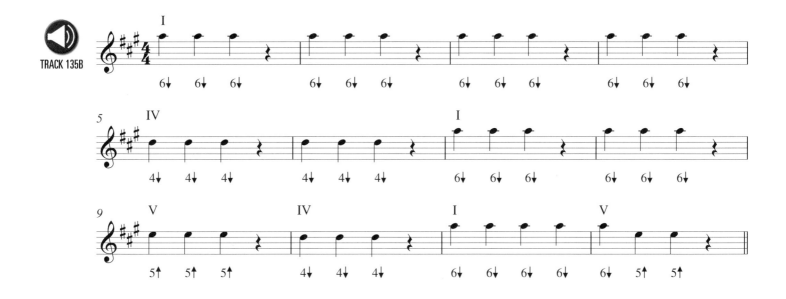

Exercise #136: Sixth Position Simplified Blues Scale (Bends: None, Position: 6th)

Again, this is the same as above, but for sixth position. Using your C harp will produce this scale and 12-bar in the key of B minor. This position is not very useful unless you can bend well, but even without bends it can play its part in the B section in an AABA chord structure. However, it won't sound like much of a scale until you can bend your 2 draw like a pro, nor will it produce a playable 12-bar, so forget about that for now.

3↓ 4↓ 5↑ 5↓ 6↓ 7↓

Exercise #137: Third Position (Simplified) Blues Scale and 12-Bar (Bends: 6, Position: 3rd)

This is an old friend from Week 9. It's one of my favorite positions, at least partly because it's not quite as commonly played as second position (cross harp). In this version, the 6 draw bend note is included to give you the real (not simplified) third position blues scale. Bend the 6 if you can; do a QRB 6 draw if you can't.

**Exercise #138: Fancier B Part of a 32-Bar AABA Jazz Solo #1
(Bends: QBRs 4 and 6, Position: 2nd)**

This entire solo is considered to be in second position, but recall what we said earlier: Sometimes you can use a different position for a single bar or two within a longer chord structure. So this eight-bar B part uses four different positions – sixth, fifth, fourth, and third – of two bars each.

TRACK 138

Note: Create your own 32-bar AABA solo, simply by playing any of the A or B parts from Weeks 22 and 23, in the correct order: Any 8-bar A part + any 8-bar A part + any 8-bar B part + any 8-bar A part = one 32-bar AABA solo.

WEEK 24

This week, we'll focus on using the 4 draw bend in riffs and solos. We'll hit the note unbent and then bend it down. We'll also hit the note bent and let it release to its unbent state. We'll slide to it, bend it down, and then slide again. In short, we'll use the 4 draw bend in many ways. If you can't yet control this important bend, spend time working on it.

Exercise #139: The Mid-Range Second Position Blues Scale
(Bends: 4 and QRB 3, Position: 2nd)

Practice going directly from the 4 draw bend to the 4 blow note without allowing the bend to release. Even harder, practice going from the 4 blow to the 4 draw bend (without hitting the unbent 4 draw).

Exercise #140: 4 Draw Bend to 3 Draw Riff #1 (Bends: 4, Position: 2nd)

Practice bending the 4 draw and then sliding to 3 draw before eventually heading down to the 2 draw. By altering the rhythm, these notes can provide lots of different riffs.

Exercise #141: 4 Draw Bend with 6 Blow Jump Riff #2 (Bends: 4, Position: 2nd)

Here's a similar riff, but with a jump from the 3 draw to the 6 blow, so be ready! When you can do it, play this one followed by Exercise #140 for a good four-bar riff (not shown).

Exercise #142: 4 Draw Bend Riff #3 (Bends: 4, Position: 2nd)

This is another useful variation with slightly different (and non-swing) rhythm, but you're welcome to play the same riff while swinging the beat.

Exercise #143: Hitting 4 Draw Bent Riff #4 (Bends: 4, Position: 2nd)

Hitting the 4 draw bent is tricky, but it's worth it. This note combination – 4 draw bend, 4 draw, 5 draw – can be heard in lots of blues and rock solos. Practice it with this simple rhythm, getting incrementally faster and faster.

Exercise #144: 4 Draw Bending Blues Scale 12-Bar Solo
(Bends: 1, 4 and QRB 3, Position: 2nd)

This example uses easy quarter-note rhythms, but has plenty of bends.

TRACK 144

Exercise #145: 4 Draw Bent Triplet Blues Scale Riff #5 (Bends: 4, Position: 2nd)

This triplet version of the 4 draw bend/4 draw/5 draw riff will come in handy later on. Play it slowly until you can hit the bends accurately and then speed it up.

TRACK 145

Exercise #146: Easy 4 Draw Bent to 3 Draw Riff #6 (Bends: 4, Position: 2nd)

Later on, we'll do similar riffs faster. Practice this both smoothly (legato) and with a staccato articulation on each 4 draw and 4 draw bent note.

TRACK 146

Exercise #147: Sliding and Bending 4 Draw Riff #7
(Bends: 4 and QRBs 3 and 3-4, Position: 2nd)

It's not too hard to slide to a note and then bend it, but when you slide to a bent note, your mouth needs to be in perfect bent-note shape. You want to bend just as you hit the note, not before – or you'll sour the notes during the slide. Notice the *glissando* symbol (slanted line) representing a fast draw slide from 1 to 4 draw. This is an alternative way to notate a slide, as compared to the one we saw first in Week 15.

TRACK 147

Back in Weeks 12-16, we worked with two-note and one-note partial bends (QRBs) using holes 3, 4, 5, and 6. Last week, we worked with full bends on the 4 draw. This week, we'll work on riffs that require full bends on holes 4 draw and 5 draw.

Exercise #148: 5 Draw Bending Riff #1 (Bends: 4, 5 and QRB 3, Position: 2nd)

Bending the 5 draw provides a mournful, minor feel to a riff or solo. It's not quite a complete half-step bend, and, according to music theory, it's not part of the second position blues scale, but it works. This simple eight-bar riff will motivate you to bend this note, and hold it bent.

Exercise #149: 5 Draw Bending Riff #2 (Bends: 4, 5 and QRB 3, Position: 2nd)

This four-bar riff uses the same notes as the previous riff, but with different rhythms. Playing Riff #1 followed by Riff #2 will provide a 12-bar solo, albeit with no turnaround. (See Exercise #150 for that.)

Exercise #150: 5 Draw and 4 Draw Bending Riff #3 (Bends: 4 and 5, Position: 2nd)

The first two bars of this four-bar riff are somewhat similar to the previous riff, but the last two bars can be used to provide a turnaround. Combine this four-bar riff with the eight-bar riff in Exercise #148 for a complete 12-bar solo with turnaround. Alternatively, you could combine the first two bars of this riff with the first two bars of the previous riff to create a new four-bar riff.

Exercise #151: 4 Draw Bend Triplet Riff #4 (Bends: 4 and QRB 3, Position: 2nd)

Play some triplet 4 draw bends followed by one bar of a swinging descending blues scale. This two-bar riff could be used in almost any 12-bar blues solo. Replace the last 2 draw with a 1 draw, and it would make a fine turnaround for a verse.

TRACK 151

Exercise #152: 5 Draw Bend Triplet Riff #5 (Bends: 5 and QRB 4, Position: 2nd)

Although this riff could be used anywhere in a 12-bar blues solo, it will work quite nicely in bars 9-10 (V–IV). Just add a two-bar turnaround!

TRACK 152

Exercise #153: Start on 4 Draw Bent Triplet Riff #6 (Bends: 4, Position: 2nd)

This riff, like the previous one, can be used during any of the I chord parts of a 12-bar solo. It will also work reasonably well during the V–IV chords of bars 9-10. To use it as a slightly unusual but effective turnaround, replace the last note (2 draw) with a 1 draw. You can jump down to the 1 draw or slide to it; either method will work. Start empty.

TRACK 153

WEEK 26

We'll hone our 6 draw bending skills and riffs this week and spend time returning to third position. Since, when we play in second position, the V chord part is kind of like being in third position for one bar, playing some serious third position blues and rock will also give us new V–IV two-bar riffs ("bridges") to use with any of our other second position riffs. Also, when playing third position, the IV chord is like being in second position for two bars. Huh? Just try it in the next solo, and you'll hear it.

Exercise #154: The Third Position Blues Scale, Descending (Bends: 6 and QRB 4, Position: 3rd)

Since it's usually easier to hit a note unbent and then bend it, rather than the opposite, practice this third position blues scale and the scale riff that follows it. Only the rhythm is different.

Exercise #155: The Third Position Blues Scale, Ascending (Bends: 6, Position: 3rd)

Practice hitting your 6 draw bent and then releasing the bend. If this is too hard right now, go on to the next solo. You won't yet need to start on a 6 draw bend.

Exercise #156: 6 Draw Bend Second Position V–IV Riff #1 (Bends: 6 and QRBs 4, 5 and 6, Position: 2nd)

The following two exercises demonstrate a few ideas for using third position-type riffs during the second position "bridge" in a 12-bar second position blues solo. Note the staccato marks; play those notes crisply.

Exercise #157: 6 Draw Bend Second Position V–IV Riff #2 (Bends: 4, 5 and 6, and QRB 6, Position: 2nd)

Here's another bridge to use in a second position 12-bar blues solo.

Exercise #158: The Third Position Bending 12-Bar Solo
(Bends: 4, 5, and 6, and QRBs 4, 5 and 6 Position: 3rd)

Although the 4 draw bend and the 5 draw bend notes are not members of the third position blues scale, they can be used in a riff or solo to add the bluesy feeling bends provide. In this slightly eerie, minor-sounding solo, we'll use a bendy version of the second position blues scale during bars 5 and 6, the iv chord, as described above.

TRACK 158

WEEK 27

HARMONICA
AEROBICS

This week, we'll begin using one of my favorite bent notes. The 2 draw note can be bent down either one half step or two half steps (a whole step), the latter being more commonly used, especially in second position blues or rock harp.

Exercise #159: First 2 Draw Bend Practice (Bends: 2, Position: 2nd)

This tried-and-true exercise is cribbed directly from my "Bending the Blues" workshops. Do it slowly, and make sure the high bars and the low bars sound the same, just an octave apart. This will ensure you are bending your 2 draw down an entire whole step (two half steps).

TRACK 159

Exercise #160: Low-End Second Position Blues Scale and Riff #1
(Bends: 1, 2 and QRB 3-4, Position: 2nd)

Being able to use the 2 draw fully bent note allows us to play a new second position blues scale. Play the simple version – just the scale, the first two bars – a few times and then add rhythm to make it a riff in the last two bars. Hit the QRB 3-4 quickly and vigorously.

TRACK 160

Exercise #161: Hitting 2 Draw Bent (Bends: 2, Position: 2nd)

The multiple 2 draw bends in this exercise will help you practice hitting the 2 draw note already bent. Keep your proper tongue placement for the bend and stop breathing for a beat to hit the difficult bend at the end of the third bar.

TRACK 161

Exercise #162: Multiple 2 Draw Bends (Bends: 2, Position: 2nd)

Make your bent 2 draw notes staccato with a forceful articulation for each bend. When you can do this exercise, see how many bent 2 draws you can play in a row. If you can play 48, which is going to require breathing from the diaphragm, you can create an entire 12-bar blues solo. But don't do it more than once for the same audience – it's only exciting the first time!

TRACK 162

Exercise #163: Low-End Blues Scale and Riff #2 (Bends: 1, 2 and QRB 3-4, Position: 2nd)

Once you can hit 2 draw bent, you can play this variation on the second position low blues scale and a riff based on it.

TRACK 163

Exercise #164: Hard Rocking 12-Bar with Bends
(Bends: 2 and QRBs 3-4 and 4-5, Position: 2nd)

This solo is an homage inspired by the great harpist, musician, writer, and philosopher Mr. John Mayall. Buy and study his recordings – and his writings, too. He was, and is, a man far ahead of his time in a plethora of ways. And, from my few brief meetings with him, he's a gentleman as well, though not one to suffer fools gladly!

TRACK 164

WEEK 28

This week, we'll add a new bend – the 3 draw note, bent down two half steps (or one whole step) – and some low end notes to the country pentatonic scale we learned in Week 18. (Review it if you haven't played it lately.) If you have not already noticed this, the bends of the 3 draw are among the most complex harmonica techniques, since three separate bent notes – one half step down, two half steps down, and three half steps down – are possible. After you've finished this week's exercises, try the country solo on page 80. You'll be ready to play the first verse of it, if not the second.

Exercise #165: Easy 3 Draw Double Bend Exercise (Bends: 2 and 3, Position: 1st)

No, it's not bluesy. But so many of us have been raised hearing the "do-re-mi" of the major scale (Week 2) that it's easy to hear. This etude will help hone your 3 draw whole-step bend abilities. Play each sequence in both a legato (smooth) and staccato way, with a quick articulation to begin each note, bent or not.

TRACK 165

Exercise #166: The Real Country Pentatonic Scale (Bends: 3, Position: 2nd)

We'll add our new note to this great scale to make it sound more exciting. Despite its name, we use the scale in blues and rock as well as country music.

TRACK 166

Exercise #167: Extending the Real Country Pentatonic Scale (Bends: 3, Position: 2nd)

Adding two low end notes to this scale – just as we did with the simplified version in Week 18 – sounds great. It is an easy way to get more mileage from this delightful and versatile scale.

TRACK 167

Exercise #168: A County Pentatonic Riff (Bends: 3, Position: 2nd)

This simple riff sounds good, especially when you add some tone effects, such as hand wah-wahs or throat vibrato. Create your own variations simply by going up and down the scale with stylistically appropriate rhythms.

TRACK 168

Exercise #169: Three More 3 Draw Bend Techniques (Bends: 3, Position: 2nd)

Starting on a 3 draw whole-step bend, releasing it to the 3 draw, and then bending it down again (and perhaps ending on a 2 draw) sounds great, as does starting on a 3 draw whole-step bend and releasing it to a 3-4 draw chord. Finally, do the same thing, but with a 3-4 draw shake.

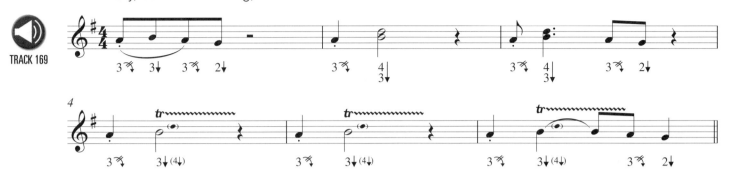

TRACK 169

Exercise #170: The Swinging Country Train (Bends: 3, Position: 2nd)

Review, if necessary, the swinging train from Week 10. Play the first bar as many times as you like – until your train has a good head of steam – then play the second bar, which gives you one silent beat to get ready for your whistle. Then use some of the preceding riffs and techniques for the whistle – Exercise #168 would work well, as would line two of Exercise #169 – before playing line two of this exercise and returning to the train. End by fading it into the distance as the train races away.

TRACK 170

The 3 draw half-step bend is more useful for second position blues than the 3 draw whole-step bend, which is commonly used in country blues and country rock, but not so much in "non-country flavored" blues or rock. This week, we'll add the 3 draw half-step bend note to our blues scales and use it in riffs. We'll also explore the technique and use of 3-4 draw bent chords and 3-4 draw and 4-5 draw trills *that bend*.

Exercise #171: Honing the 3 Draw Half-Step Bend (Bends: 3, Position: 2nd)

It's easy to over-bend or under-bend this note, but this exercise will allow you to hear the difference. When played correctly, it provides a sense of tension and excitement to a second position blues riff or solo that can't be beat! Listen to the following examples before you try them.

TRACK 171A

The first two-bar riff above has a tense, bluesy, feeling, as the 3 draw is bent down just far enough. These next two bars don't sound very bluesy – the 3 draw is not bent at all.

TRACK 171B

And these last two bars don't sound bluesy at all; they sound "wrong," if anything. The 3 draw is bent too far, like the 3 draw double bend of a country scale. It's fine for country, but not so good for blues.

TRACK 171C

Exercise #172: The Real Second Position Blues Scale #1 (Bends: 3 and 4, Position: 2nd)

This is the last note required to play a true blue blues scale. Up until now, we've been using the QRB 3 draw half-step bend; now it's time for the real thing. Hold that 3 draw bent – make sure it's one half step.

TRACK 172

Exercise #173: The Real Second Position Blues Scale #2 (Bends: 1, 2 and 3, Position: 2nd)

This one is even "bendier," but sounds great. Make those bends clear and crisp.

TRACK 173

Exercise #174: Real Second Position Blues Riff #1 (Bends: 2, 3 and 4, Position: 2nd)

Now that you know the entire, real second position blues scale, you can create an unlimited number of riffs similar to this one. Hold that long 3 draw bend steady.

TRACK 174

Exercise #175: Real Second Position Blues Riff #2 (Bends: 2, 3 and 4, and QRB 4, Position: 2nd)

This one is a little harder, with more bends and more complex timing. Use it anywhere in a blues solo, or replace the last 2 draw note of bar 4 with another 1 draw – for an excellent riff on the last four bars of a 12-bar blues solo with turnaround.

TRACK 175

Exercise #176: Real Second Position Blues Riff #3 (Bends: 3 and QRBs 3-4 and 4, Position: 2nd)

This one has a few pickup notes that begin before the main bar starts, so begin playing after a count of three. Starting a trill with a QRB is a great harp technique, so use it frequently.

TRACK 176

Exercise #177: Real 3-4 Chord Bend Turnaround (Bends: 2 and 3-4, Position: 2nd)

Little Walter, Big Walter, James Cotton – everyone uses a turnaround with the 3-4 draw bend on some of their blues verses. So should you! In the later solos, we'll end verses with variations of this. Get your mouth and tongue into the exact correct place to play a 3 draw half-step bend, but keep your lips open to enclose the 3-4 draw chord. It takes lots of wind and tongue/lip strength. This exercise will help. The first two bars are for practice; the last two bars are the actual I–V turnaround.

TRACK 177

Exercise #178: Using a 3 Draw Bend in IV Chord Riffs (Bends: 3 and QRB 4, Position: 2nd)

In second positions, our IV chord riffs have tended to lack pizzazz – until now, when we can add the 3 draw half-step bend. Go back to Week 14 and revitalize the IV chord of your second position rock backbeat IV chord riffs, like this.

TRACK 178

Exercise #179: The 3 Draw Half-Step to 3 Draw Whole-Step Bend Riff
(Bends: 3, Position: 1st, 2nd, or 5th)

This complex bent-note sequence can be used in first, second, or fifth positions. Practice it slowly and carefully. The version below would probably fit best in a fifth position solo or riff. By changing the last note of the third bar (2 blow) to a 2 draw (Variation B), you can make it fit perfectly into a second position riff. By changing that last note to a 1 draw (Variation C), you create an excellent, if somewhat dark-sounding, second position turnaround.

TRACK 179A

TRACK 179B

TRACK 179C

Exercise #180: Bending Your Trills
(Bends: 3-4 and 4-5, and QRBs 3-4 and 4-5, Position: 1st, 2nd, or 5th)

If you've practiced your 3-4 draw chord half-step bend, this will be easy. If not, jump back two exercises. Practice bending your 4-5 draw chord also, then try these bending trills. When you think you have the hang of it, listen to Magic Dick's world-class trill bending (using 3-4 draw) on the J. Geils Band's rock classic "Whammer Jammer" – and kneel in awe.

TRACK 180

We've avoided playing first position blues up until now for a reason: If you can't bend your low-end notes well, first position blues sounds… un-bluesy. Now that we can use the 2 draw whole-step bend and the 3 draw half-step bend, we're almost ready. Also, this week, we'll use the 2 draw half-step bend. Many good players – including famous ones – either don't know or never use this bend. However, knowing it will make your first position blues much more interesting. Soon you'll have a chance to play an exciting solo verse using the scales and riffs from this week and the next.

Exercise #181: Simplified First Position Blues Scale (Bends: 2 and 3, Position: 1st)

Go up and down this scale until you feel ready to add rhythm and octave blocking. Yes, the second note *should* be bent down a half step, but if you can bend the 2 blow and make it sound good, hats off to you!

TRACK 181

Exercise #182: Easy First Position Blues Riff #1 (Bends: 2 and 3, Position: 1st)

Jump cleanly from the single notes to the octave blocks and this will sound fine – even without the 2 draw whole-step bend. You can swing the eighth notes in bar 2 or not; it sounds good either way.

TRACK 182

Exercise #183: Another "Easy" First Position Blues Riff #2 (Bends: 3, Position: 1st)

The first bar of this riff can be used as the basis for an entire first position 12-bar blues solo. It also can be used during the IV chord part of a second position blues solo. (Remember that when playing a 12-bar solo in a particular position, other position scales and riffs can often be used briefly during certain specific chords of that solo. For more on this subject, see my book *Blues & Rock Harmonica Made Easy* (Hal Leonard).

Note: Since 3 blow and 2 draw provide the exact same note, you can use whichever you please when you see a note symbol on the second line from the bottom of the staff. When I want to go smoothly from an out note to that second staff line note, I generally use 3 blow. When I want to go smoothly from another draw note to that note, I use 2 draw. It's your call, so do what feels easiest or smoothest to you. Try it both ways, below.

TRACK 183

Exercise #184: Another "Easy" First Position Blues Riff #3 (Bends: 2 and 3, Position: 1st)

Here's another riff, based on the second bar of Exercise #183 above, that can be used as the basis for an entire first position 12-bar blues solo. It offers a good opportunity to practice lots of jumping from an octave block to a bend – a useful skill indeed.

Exercise #185: Easy First Position IV Chord Riff (Bends: QRB 6, Position: 1st)

In first position, the IV chord is the hardest part. (It's based on the rarely used and brutally difficult 12th position blues scale.) However, by leaving out the hardest of the 12th position notes, we can play an easy but okay-sounding IV chord riff in the mid-range. Later on, we'll do a harder solo verse in first position, with low end and high end, bend-filled IV chord parts. The V chord parts of a first position blues solo are based on second position, so those bars will be easy – or at least they'll look familiar.

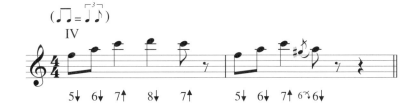

Exercise #186: Almost Real First Position Blues Scale (Bends: 2 and 3, Position: 1st)

There's no easy way to bend the 2 blow note. You can flatten it a bit by clamping down on it with the lips and tongue, but other than that, this is the most complete low-end first position blues scale. The half-step bent 2 draw is a tough bend to perfect, so keep working on it.

Exercise #187: Hard First Position Triplet Practice (Bends: 2, Position: 1st)

Practice hitting the 2 draw fully bent as the beginning of a triplet. You'll hear this note combination in lots of first position blues solos.

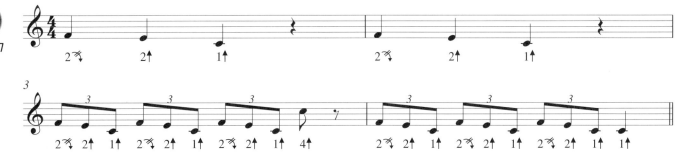

Exercise #188: Hard First Position Blues Scale Riff (Bends: 2 and 3, Position: 1st)

Play with the rhythm and note order to make a riff, admittedly a hard one, from the previous scale.

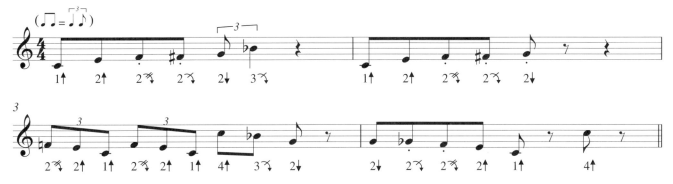

71

Now we'll attack – and "attack" is the right word, since these are notes we'll use quite aggressively – the high-end first position blues scale. To do this, we'll need to blow bend the holes 8, 9, and 10. The first position blues options are somewhat limited in the mid-range for all but the most technical players, but they're great at the low end (as you saw in the last week) and even better when you can use the high-end notes.

These days, I'm able to get over 50 percent of my week-long beginning workshop students to blow bend at least one of these holes. It took *me* four and a half years to figure out blow bending. That's four years after I first heard blow bends in the work of the superb rock harpist Magic Dick and the blues of the great Jimmy Reed. Through the kindness and generosity of West Coast country harpist Jerry (not Jimmy) Reed, I was able to understand "what the heck those guys were doing up in the high end."

Blow bending is likely to reduce the longevity of your harmonica. The better you get at it, the more softly you can do it and the less damaging it will be. Because blow bending is easier to learn on – and less likely to damage – a lower-key harmonica, we will now switch to a key of A ten-hole harmonica.

Since the harmonica is transposable simply by switching to another key of harp, we'll keep the notation written in the key of C throughout. When the key of A harp is needed, you'll see "Transpose C = A" before the example. Notation-wise, you'll do just what you've been doing, but with your A harp; it will sound three half steps lower. If you don't see the "Transpose C = A" indication before an exercise, continue to use your key of C harp.

Exercise #189: Blow Bending the 10 Riff (Bends: 10, Position: 1st)

Although two blow bends are available from the 10 blow note, the half-step 10 blow bend is much less commonly used than the "pretty-much-two-half-steps" 10 blow bend. FYI, the "pretty-much-two-half-steps" bends on 10 blow and 9 blow are actually more like "one-and-a-half-step" bends – but they work well and sound good. The notation may look scary, but the bends are harder. Good luck! (If you can't do this, I recommend *Bending the Blues*, available from Hal Leonard.)

TRACK 189

Transpose: C = A

Exercise #190: Blow Bending the 9 Riff (Bends: 9 and QRB 9, Position: 1st)

Generally, the 9 blow whole-step bend is more useful than the half-step version. However, sometimes a blow bend is used for dramatic effect, and how far it's bent is not always important. Even a QRB on the 9 blow can be a powerful note in a solo.

TRACK 190

Transpose: C = A

Exercise #191: Starting on a 9 Bent Blow Riff #1 (Bends: 9, Position: 1st)

It's important to be able to begin a note bent and then release it up to its unbent sound. Notice that each of the faster two-note riffs begins with an articulation, as indicated by the accent symbol.

TRACK 191

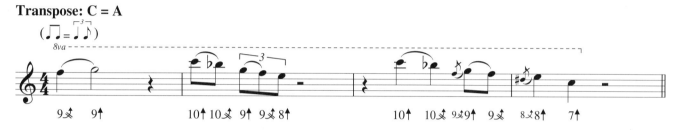

Exercise #192: Starting on a 9 Bent Blow Riff #2
(Bends: 9 and 10, and QRBs 8 and 9, Position: 1st)

This one's pretty hard, even with a simpler rhythm. If you can do it accurately, you're in pretty good blow bending shape.

TRACK 192

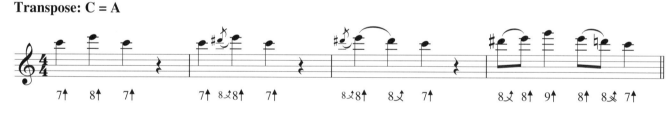

Exercise #193: 8 Half-Step Blow Bend Riff (Bends: 8 and QRB 8, Position: 1st)

Although the 8 blow note can be bent down to produce almost the same note as the 8 draw, it's the half-step 8 blow bend that is most often used. It provides a crucial note in the first position blues scale, which we'll work on after you practice this exercise. We'll also use this note in the fourth position high-end blues scale in Week 32.

TRACK 193

Exercise #194: High-End First Position Blues Scale #1 (Bends: 8, 9, and 10, Position: 1st)

There are two ways to play this scale. In today's exercise, we'll use the 9 draw note, which probably will be more accurate in terms of pitch. Playing blow bends tends to cause "saliva blocks" on high draw notes. (This is when a bit of saliva prevents a reed from playing freely until it is shaken out, blown out, or dried out.) The 8 blow bend provides the first position blues scale note we wish we could get from the 2 blow "bend."

TRACK 194

73

Exercise #195: High-End First Position Blues Scale #2 (Bends: 8, 9 and 10, Position: 1st)

In this second way, we'll use the whole-step 9 blow bend instead of the 9 draw note. You may think it sounds "bluesier." It's your choice on this, so try it both ways.

Exercise #196: High-End First Position Blues Riff (Bends: 8, 9, and 10, Position: 1st)

Add some rhythmic variety and turn that scale into a riff, like this. Make up your own, too.

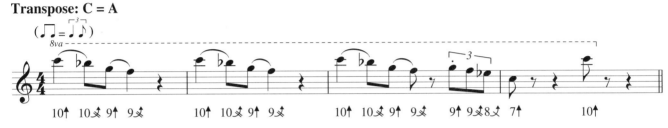

If you can play these scales and exercises – or even if you can't, yet – go to page 88 and read about the first position blues solo.

Our last bend will be a difficult and unusual one: the 3 draw triple half-step bend. It's used mostly in third position low-end blues; many harpists never play it. But we will, for the same reason British mountaineer George Mallory wanted to climb Mount Everest: "Because it is there." And for that reason, we'll also learn to play real fourth, fifth, and sixth position blues scales this week, then later use them in solos. Remember: To know which key harp to use for which position, see the chart on page 93.

With the exception of Exercise #201, these etudes utilize a key of C harmonica.

Exercise #197: High/Low Third Position Blues Scale, Descending (Bends: 2, 3 and 6, Position: 3rd)

There's no easy way to learn the bending needed for the low-end third position blues scale, except to memorize what the higher version sounds like and then try to replicate it using low-end bends. Some students, when playing this is a downward direction, prefer to use 3 blow instead of 2 draw; it's your call. The master harpist Charlie Musselwhite is a wonderful model to listen to for this type of playing.

TRACK 197

Exercise #198: High/Low Third Position Blues Scale, Ascending (Bends: 2, 3 and 6, Position: 3rd)

Question: Which is easier: going down or going up? Answer: Neither. Just keep working on it.

TRACK 198

Exercise #199: Low Third Position Blues Riff (Bends: 2 and 3, Position: 3rd)

When you can play this riff, you'll be ready to play the third position solos in the following weeks. Slowly is fine, and probably necessary. Notice the one-beat pickup note that precedes the first bar. Good luck and keep trying.

TRACK 199

Exercise #200: Fourth Position Mid- and Low-Blues Scales (Bends: 3, Position: 4th)

Fourth position is good for playing minor-flavored blues and will also help you create better V chord parts for your third position solos. (When playing in third position, the V chord puts you in fourth position.) I discussed this when we learned the rock ballad in Week 19 (when we used fifth position for one bar of the ballad solo). Familiarize yourself with this plaintive scale. You can use your C or A harp here and in Exercise #201 – the highest blow bend, on 8 blow, won't be too high when played on either key harp.

TRACK 200

Exercise #201: Fourth Position High-End Blues Scale (Bends: 8, Position: 4th)

Yes, this is stratospheric and quite challenging. You may not use it often, but it's worth knowing about, since it's the only realistic way to get the "missing" fourth position blues scale note. (The other option is mid-range overblowing, which is not a good idea because it wrecks harps too quickly.) The audio track features the A harp, since that 8 blow bend is a bit easier.

TRACK 201

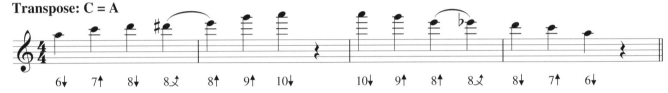

Exercise #202: Fifth Position Blues Scales (Bends: 3, Position: 5th)

This is good practice for mastering the difficult 3 draw whole-step bend and 3 draw half-step bend sequence. It's also useful for the vi chords in second position chord structures – such as the rock ballad, or as two bars of the "B" part in the 32-bar AABA jazz structure in Week 23. Use the 2 draw or 3 blow note – whichever feels easier to you. I often use 2 draw going up and 3 blow going down, as shown.

TRACK 202

Exercise #203: Alternate Fifth Position Blues Scale/Riff (Bends: 3, Position: 5th)

Unlike the previous example, this scale version is completed in the lower octave; the riff that follows does the same.

TRACK 203

Exercise #204: Sixth Position Blues Scale (Bends: 2 and 3, Position: 6th)

Use this scale when improvising over the III chord in the "B" part of a 32-bar AABA form. It's also good practice for going from the 2 draw whole-step bend to the 2 draw half-step bend to the 3 draw whole-step bend, and vice versa.

TRACK 204

ABOUT WEEKS 33–42 (THE "SOLO" WEEKS)

These solos come in many positions and a number of styles using various chord progressions. If you've been able to play most of the exercises and riffs and solos this far, you're in great shape to start playing any of them.

But even if you can't bend well or are a bit shaky on some of the rhythms, you'll be able to play the earlier verses of certain solos, since the earlier solos progress in difficulty from beginning to end – and some of them get quite difficult toward the end of the solo.

In case you need some review, we'll indicate when a solo relates to specific material in an earlier week.

Important (Especially for Near-Beginners)

Even if these solos seem ridiculously difficult to you now, take time to read about them as you listen to the audio tracks and look at the notation. It's important to know what is possible, to know how different positions and styles sound, and to have an idea (from the notation) of the notes and bends that are used. All this will have a tremendously beneficial effect on the development of your playing.

WEEK 33

Exercise #205: Two-Bar Funk Rock Solo (Position: 2nd, Level: Moderately Easy to Difficult)

This long solo is based on the two-bar funk rock chord structure introduced on page 8. It begins with easier material meant to reflect the chords used in this progression. These earlier measures use some or most of the second position blues scale during the I chord bars, and some or most of the first position blues scale during the IV chords.

The solo then goes on to feature longer sequences of notes that don't correlate as closely to the changing of the chords. The phrases of this second type are based mostly on the second position blues scale, with occasional notes or sequences from the first position blues scale thrown in – usually, but not always, during the IV chords.

TRACK 205

78

WEEK 34

Exercise #206: Four-Bar Three-Chord Rhythm and Blues Verses)
Position: 2nd, Level: Moderately Easy, Moderate, and Difficult)

This three-chord structure, with each phrase two bars long, can be used to play either rock or R&B music. You can hear its echo in songs such as "Hang On Sloopy," "Louie Louie," and "Wild Thing," as well as hundreds of lesser-known tunes.

In my weeklong *Mindfulness Through Music*™ workshops, I call the most basic version of this lovely chord progression (page 8) The HarMantra™, because it's so relaxing and pleasant. Of course, when you get to the harder phrases – and especially the one with lots of blow bends – it may not seem quite so calming. Notice the triplet pickup at the beginning.

TRACK 206

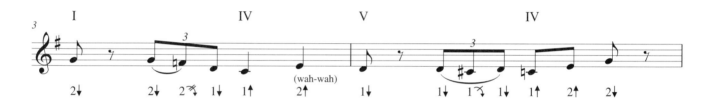

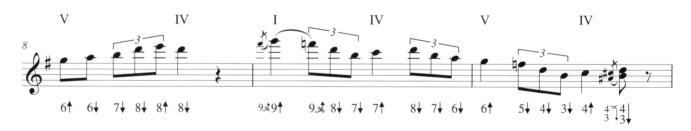

Exercise #207: Country Eight-Bar Solo
(Position: 2nd, Level: Moderate and Moderately Difficult)

It's fun, lively, and easy to play along with. This eight-bar chord structure can be heard in lots of country and country blues tunes. If you've been practicing your 3 draw bends, the first verse of this solo should be relatively easy. The second verse is harder and includes some blow bends. If you like this style of music, check out *How to Play Country and Western Harmonica* (HL14015466), which covers the use of the high end of the harmonica in country and rock playing.

TRACK 207

Exercise #208: Boogie Woogie Bends Solo (Position: 2nd, Level: Moderately Difficult)

Here's a simple take – using lots of bends – on a classic 12-bar blues style: the boogie woogie. It might be useful to review the easier boogie woogie 12-bar on page 16 before attempting this solo, which uses more complex notes and bends (of course). The triplet bends in bar 11 will require some practice time. But except for these, we might rate the level as merely "Moderate."

TRACK 208

Exercise #209: Third-Position Rock Solo (Position: 3rd, Level: Moderately Difficult)

Most rock harmonica music is played in second or cross position. Playing a rock solo in third position, then, will surprise and entertain your listeners with its eerie and driving feel, while building important bending and timing skills. If this one seems at all confusing or difficult, listening to (and practicing) the simple third-position rock solo in Week 9 (page 27, Exercise #56) will help.

TRACK 209

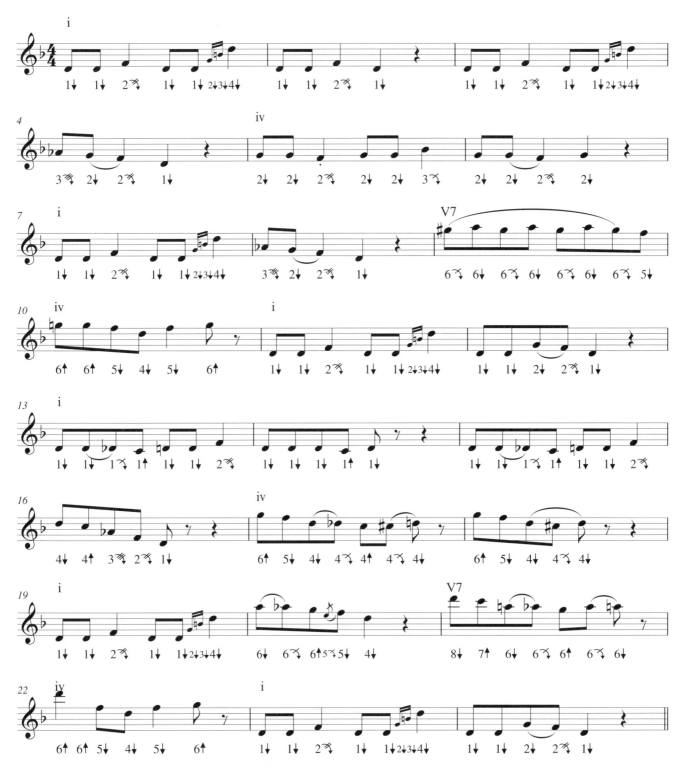

Exercise #210: Slow 12-Bar Blues with Intro and Ending
(Position: 2nd, Difficult Level: Moderately Difficult)

The first verse of a blues is often preceded by a two- or four-bar introduction ("intro"). This intro is usually similar to the last four or two bars of a standard 12-bar blues verse. For slow blues songs, a four-bar intro like the one below is customary.

The ending, sometimes called the "outro," is usually a sequence of notes ending on the main note ("tonic") of the song, in this case a 2 draw note. The ending of this solo is an homage to Marion "Little Walter" Jacobs, reversing the note order of one of my favorite Little Walter endings.

In this solo, as is often done in slower blues songs, the second bar of the main verse is changed from the usual I chord to a IV chord. The introduction starts with four pickup notes on the upbeat of beat 3. The bends in bar 13 will be hard if you haven't practiced your low-end third position blues scale (page 75). The ending will be hard if you haven't worked on your 2 draw bends.

TRACK 210

Exercise #211: Four-Bar Rock Ballad Solo (Position: 2nd, Level: Moderate and Difficult)

This classic 1950s style of rock music, first introduced in Week 19 and best exemplified by the classic rock ballad "Duke of Earl," has a lovely, flowing, romantic and soulful feeling. As with other solos, this set of two verses, four bars each in length, are not necessarily how I would choose to play a four-bar rock ballad solo. Rather, each of the two verses represents a different approach to playing this lovely, early rock 'n' roll chord structure. You need not play this as I do. Instead, use it as a jumping off point to create similar solo verses of your own.

TRACK 211

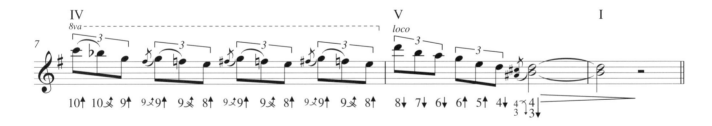

Exercise #212: Swinging Blues Rock Train Solo (Position: 2nd, Level: Easy to Difficult)

The long solo on page 86 is based on the train chord pattern introduced on page 28. We fancy up the basic train pattern in various ways and introduce "whistle" sections using notes mostly from the blues scale. The introduction, the hardest part, is an homage to "Whammer Jammer" by the J. Geils Band, with harmonica by Magic Dick. Every harp player should own at least their first three albums: *The J. Geils Band* (1970), *The Morning After* (1971), and the live album *"Live" Full House* (1972). The first of these was my initial exposure to rock harp, courtesy of Mr. Van Stavern.

Since we harpists usually play a train without other musical accompaniment, we can play it using any key harmonica. However, the high blow bends are likely to be easier on a low harp like A (which is what I use in the recording) than on a C or higher pitched instrument. But try playing a solo train on any key harp that you have! If you should want to play a train like this with other musicians, your A harp will produce a train in the key of E, and your C harp will produce a train in the key of G. It is played in standard cross or second position harmonica, in other words.

Note the bar of silence after the intro before the train starts. Tap your foot or nod your head once per beat during this to help your listeners get the basic underlying beat of the train as it clacks its way down the track.

Once you've learned the basic train variations that represent the clacking of the train wheels, and a few riffs to use for train whistles, you can combine them to make up trains of your own. Generally, I allow my train to speed up or slow down as it will. That's why the audio recording of the second train example – faster and more "free form" – is livelier than that of the first example, which is played along with a metronome and written out in standard notation.

WEEK 41

Example #213: 32-Bar Jazz AABA Solo (Position: 2nd, Level: Moderately Difficult)

This second-position solo is composed of fancier (and bendier) versions of the A and B parts from Weeks 22 and 23. Reviewing the exercises in those weeks will help you with this. If you're practicing each A part and B part separately, notice the pickup notes – three eighth notes (1 draw, 2 blow, 1 draw) – that precede each of the A parts. It is part of the bar (the last three eighth notes) before each A part starts, but it's also the beginning of that A part. Flow these pickup notes right into the first real bar of the A part that follows.

The chord symbols above each line in this solo sketch out the simplest possible 32-bar AABA chord progression. But once you learn to play this solo – and even improvise your own – you'll find it possible to maneuver your way through more complex variations of this form. Practice the simpler versions mentioned above as well as this one, then make up your own using the suggestions in Weeks 22 and 23.

TRACK 213

Exercise #214: First Position 12-Bar Blues Solo
(Position: 1st, Level: Moderately Difficult and Advanced)

The first solo of this verse requires lots of low-end bending, while the second verse – although the rhythm is relatively simple – requires both low- and high-end bends. Listen to this solo several times, following the notation with your eyes and your mind, before you try it.

TRACK 214

Transpose: C = A

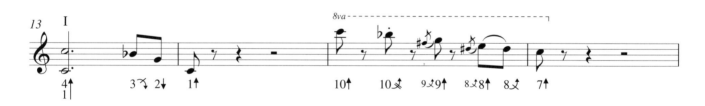

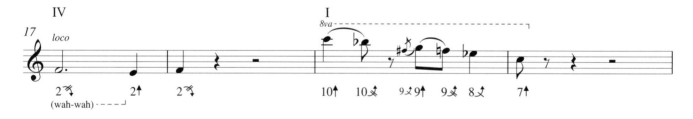

READING RHYTHMS

All the exercises in this book have a 4/4 time signature. This means there are four beats per measure ("bar"), and a quarter note gets one beat. Here are the corresponding notes and values for 4/4 time.

𝅝   whole note = 4 beats

𝅗𝅥•   dotted-half note = 3 beats

𝅗𝅥   half note = 2 beats

𝅘𝅥•   dotted-quarter note = 1½ beats

𝅘𝅥   quarter note = 1 beat

𝅘𝅥𝅮•   dotted-eighth note = ¾ beat

𝅘𝅥𝅮   eighth note = ½ beat

𝅘𝅥𝅯   16th note = ¼ beat

When you read rhythmic notation, you're relating the written notes to the beat. The first step is to recognize the various note values, as shown above. The chart that follows shows the relative value of notes. As you can see, eighth notes have single flags (little "tails" attached to the top of the note stem) or beams (horizontal lines that connect the tops of note stems), while 16th notes have double flags or beams. Some are flagged while others are beamed; this doesn't affect their duration.

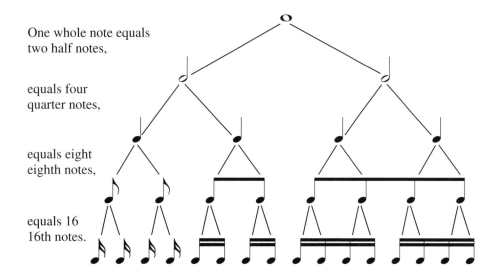

One whole note equals two half notes,

equals four quarter notes,

equals eight eighth notes,

equals 16 16th notes.

Below are the rests commonly encountered in 4/4 time. Their durations are the sames as that of their corresponding notes.

A quarter-note *triplet* is a rhythmic device that indicates three equally spaced notes within one beat. Think of a three-syllable word like "strawberry." Tap your foot in a steady rhythm, and for each tap say "straw-ber-ry." Make sure each syllable is the same length.

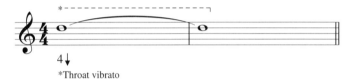

"straw-ber - ry"

Ties allow us to continue holding a note across a bar line, as in Exercise #50, where two whole notes are tied to each other, for a total of eight beats.

4↓
*Throat vibrato

They also enable us to lengthen a note within a measure, as in Exercise #88.

HARMONICA CHARTS

The Notes of the C Diatonic (Ten Hole) Harmonica

Hole #:	1	2	3	4	5	6	7	8	9	10
Exhale:	C	E	G	C	E	G	C	E	G	C
Inhale:	D	G	B	D	F	A	B	D	F	A
Commonly Used Bends	---------------inhaled bends---------------							--exhaled bends--		
	Db	Gb	Bb	Db	E*	Ab		Eb	Gb	B
		F	A						F	Bb
			Ab							

* This note is a useable bend, but is very difficult to bend down all the way to E.

The Notes of the A Diatonic (Ten Hole) Harmonica

Hole #:	1	2	3	4	5	6	7	8	9	10
Exhale:	A	C♯	E	A	C♯	E	A	C♯	E	A
Inhale:	B	E	G♯	B	D	F♯	G#	B	D	F#
Commonly Used Bends	---------------inhaled bends---------------							--exhaled bends--		
	Bb	Eb	G	Bb	Db*	F		C	Eb	Ab
		D	Gb						D	G
			F							

* This note is a useable bend, but is very difficult to bend down all the way to Db.

COMMONLY USED HARMONICA POSITIONS

As mentioned in the book, it is crucial to know which key of harmonica to use when playing along with a particular style and key of music. The relationship between the key of the harmonica and the key of the music is often called the "position" of the harmonica.

There are three commonly used positions, three less common ones, and six more possible positions that are rarely used. The following charts cover these six common and less common positions.

First (also called "Straight") Position is most commonly used when playing major scale melodies, and is sometimes used for playing blues. The key of the music is the same as the key of the harp.

Music Key:	C	C♯/Db	D	D♯/Eb	E	F	F♯/Gb	G	G♯/Ab	A	A♯/Bb	B
Harp Key:	C	C♯/Db	D	D♯/Eb	E	F	F♯/Gb	G	G♯/Ab	A	A♯/Bb	B

Second (also called "Cross") Position is the most commonly used position when playing blues and rock music.

Music Key:	G	G♯/Ab	A	A♯/Bb	B	C	C♯/Db	D	D♯/Eb	E	F	F♯/Gb
Harp Key:	C	C♯/Db	D	D♯/Eb	E	F	F♯/Gb	G	G♯/Ab	A	A♯/Bb	B

Third (also called "Dorian Mode") Position is commonly used when playing Dorian scale melodies, and is often used for playing minor scale blues (though it can also be used to play non-minor blues).

Music Key:	Dm	D#m/Ebm	Em	Fm	F#m/Gbm	Gm	G#m/Abm	Am	A#m/Bbm	Bm	Cm	C#m/Dbm
Harp Key:	C	C#/Db	D	D#/Eb	E	F	F#/Gb	G	G#/Ab	A	A#/Bb	B

LESS COMMONLY USED HARMONICA POSITIONS

The following three positions are rarely used, but worth knowing for more advanced players. They are described in more detail in Week 32.

Fourth Position (another minor-flavored position, can be used in some blues, rock, and jazz music, and many Aeolian mode melodies).

Music Key:	Am	A#m/Bbm	Bm	Cm	C#m/Dbm	Dm	D#m/Ebm	Em	Fm	F#m/Gbm	Gm	G#m/Abm
Harp Key:	C	C#/Db	D	D#/Eb	E	F	F#/Gb	G	G#/Ab	A	A#/Bb	B

Note: There is some controversy amongst harp players as to whether this position should be known as fourth or fifth position. Some older harmonica methods call this fifth position. In keeping with standard music "Circle of Fifths" theory, fourth position is a more appropriate name.

Fifth Position (in this method book mostly used for playing vi chord accompaniment). Music theorists call this Phrygian mode.

Music Key:	E	F	F#/Gb	G	G#/Ab	A	A#/Bb	B	C	C#/Db	D	D#/Eb
Harp Key:	C	C#/Db	D	D#/Eb	E	F	F#/Gb	G	G#/Ab	A	A#/Bb	B

Sixth Position (in this method book mostly used for playing iii chord accompaniment). Music theorists call this Locrian mode.

Music Key:	B	C	C#/Db	D	D#/Eb	E	F	F#/Gb	G	G#/Ab	A	A#/Bb
Harp Key:	C	C#/Db	D	D#/Eb	E	F	F#/Gb	G	G#/Ab	A	A#/Bb	B

THE SIX HARMONICA POSITIONS
Music Key and Harp Key Chart

Position: First ("Straight")

Music Key:	C	C#	D	D#	E	F	F#	G	G#	A	A#	B
Harp Key:	C	C#	D	D#	E	F	F#	G	G#	A	A#	B

Note: First position harp is most often used to play major key melodies, but if you can bend well it can be used used to play any style of music.

Position: Second ("Cross")

Music Key:	C	C#	D	D#	E	F	F#	G	G#	A	A#	B
Harp Key:	F	F#	G	G#	A	A#	B	C	C#	D	D#	E

Note: This is the most common position for playing blues and rock harmonica music.

Position: Third

Music Key:	Cm	C#m	Dm	D#m	Em	Fm	F#m	Gm	G#m	Am	A#m	Bm
Harp Key:	A#	B	C	C#	D	D#	E	F	F#	G	G#	A

Note: Third position harp is most often, though not always, played with minor or blues music.

Position: Fourth

Music Key:	Cm	C#m	Dm	D#m	Em	Fm	F#m	Gm	G#m	Am	A#m	Bm
Harp Key:	D#	E	F	F#	G	G#	A	A#	B	C	C#	D

Note: Like Third Position, Fourth position harp is often played along with minor key music.

Position: Fifth

Music Key:	C	C#	D	D#	E	F	F#	G	G#	A	A#	B
Harp Key:	G#	A	A#	B	C	C#	D	D#	E	F	F#	G

Note: Fifth position harp is most often used to play a portion of a jazz song. It is rarely used to play an entire song by itself, although you can do it if you like!

Position: Sixth

Music Key:	C	C#	D	D#	E	F	F#	G	G#	A	A#	B
Harp Key:	C#	D	D#	E	F	F#	G	G#	A	A#	B	C

Note: Like Fifth position, Sixth position harp is most often used to play only a portion of a song. It's hard to play an entire blues or other song in this position. Try doing it if you don't believe me.

HARMONICA NOTATION LEGEND

Harmonica music can be notated two different ways: on a *musical staff*, and in *tablature*.

THE MUSICAL STAFF shows pitches and rhythms and is divided by bar lines into measures. Pitches are named after the first seven letters of the alphabet.

TABLATURE graphically represents the harmonica music. Each note will be accompanied by a number, 1 through 10, indicating what hole you are to play. The arrow that follows indicates whether to blow or draw. (All examples are shown using a C diatonic harmonica.)

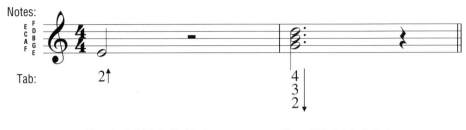

Notes:

Tab: 2↑

Blow (exhale) into 2nd hole.

4
3
2

Draw (inhale) 2nd, 3rd, & 4th holes together.

Notes on the C Harmonica

Exhaled (Blown) Notes

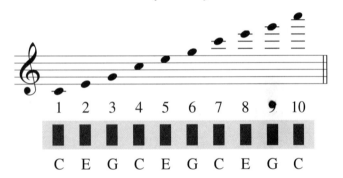

1	2	3	4	5	6	7	8	9	10
C	E	G	C	E	G	C	E	G	C

Inhaled (Drawn) Notes

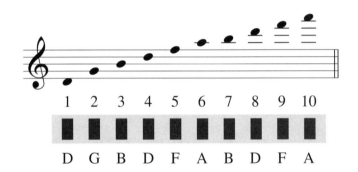

1	2	3	4	5	6	7	8	9	10
D	G	B	D	F	A	B	D	F	A

Bends

Blow Bends		**Draw Bends**	
♪	• 1/4 step	♪	• 1/4 step
♪	• 1/2 step	♪	• 1/2 step
♪	• 1 step	♪	• 1 step
♪	• 1 1/2 steps	♪	• 1 1/2 steps

Definitions for Special Harmonica Notation

SLURRED BEND: Play (draw) 3rd hole, then bend the note down one whole step.

GRACE NOTE BEND: Starting with a pre-bent note, immediately release bend to the target note.

VIBRATO: Begin adding vibrato to the sustained note on beat 3.

TONGUE BLOCKING: Using your tongue to block holes 2 & 3, play octaves on holes 1 & 4.

TRILL: Shake the harmonica rapidly to alternate between notes.

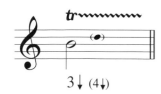

NOTE: Tablature numbers in parentheses are used when:
- The note is sustained, but a new articulation begins (such as vibrato), or
- The quantity of notes being sustained changes, or
- A change in dynamics (volume) occurs.
- It's the alternate note in a trill.

Additional Musical Definitions

D.S. al Coda

- Go back to the sign (𝄋), then play until the measure marked "***To Coda***," then skip to the section labelled "**Coda**."

D.C. al Fine

- Go back to the beginning of the song and play until the measure marked "***Fine***" (end).

- Repeat measures between signs.

(accent)
- Accentuate the note (play initial attack louder).

(staccato)
- Play the note short.

- When a repeated section has different endings, play the first ending only the first time and the second ending only the second time.

Dynamics

p
- Piano (soft)

mp
- Mezzo Piano (medium soft)

mf
- Mezzo Forte (medium loud)

f
- Forte (loud)

(crescendo)
- Gradually louder

(decrescendo)
- Gradually softer

ABOUT THE AUTHOR

More than a million people have used David Harp's wide variety of blues, rock, country, and folk harmonica instruction methods, as well as his methods for music theory, and for other instruments. But as a child, David was far from a prodigy. Given a cello (the perfect instrument for a nerdy, pudgy, introverted ten-year-old boy), his unwillingness to learn standard musical notation, coupled with his beloved cat's "accidental" destruction of that fine instrument, convinced him that he was tone deaf.

Nine years later, the accidental acquisition of a ten-hole harmonica at the beginning of a lengthy hitch-hiking trip changed his mind. Soon afterward, David discovered blues and rock harp music (see Dedication), and he was sold on the "tin sandwich." After completing a B.A. in psychology, David began to study pedagogy (the science of how to teach), and applied that knowledge to become the San Francisco Bay Area's best-known harmonica teacher. He considers his niche to be "making simple what other teachers make complicated."

Since receiving his master's degree in 1988 (specializing in organizational psychology and mindfulness studies) David has combined his two main interests – psychology and harmonica – to create unique group presentations using that humble instrument to teach mindfulness, team-building, and stress reduction to organizations ranging in size from a few dozen to a few thousand, and ranging in type from Ben & Jerry's Ice Cream to the FBI (also including companies such as Merck Pharmaceutical, the Blue Cross, the Red Cross, and Kraft Foods). He also does similar volunteer work with groups of at-risk kids, frail elderly folk, environmental and veteran groups, and people who are terminally ill.

David offers customized private lessons via phone and Skype for both harmonica and mindfulness students of any level, from total beginner to pro.